MW01173323

Joshua

LIVING THE VICTORIOUS LIFE

FRAZER 365

Joshua

Living the Victorious Life

Frazer Discipleship

Copyright © 2024 by Frazer Discipleship. All rights reserved.

No part of this book may be reproduced in any form or by any electronic or mechanical means, including information storage and retrieval systems, without written permission from the author, except for the use of brief quotations in a book review.

Unless otherwise noted, Scripture quotations are from the ESV® Bible (The Holy Bible, English Standard Version®), copyright © 2001 by Crossway Bibles, a publishing ministry of Good News Publishers. Used by permission. All rights reserved.

Scripture quotations marked NIV are taken from the Holy Bible, New International Version®, NIV®. Copyright © 1973, 1978, 1984, 2011 by Biblica, Inc.TM Used by permission of Zondervan. All rights reserved worldwide. www.zondervan.comThe "NIV" and "New International Version" are trademarks registered in the United States Patent and Trademark Office by Biblica, Inc.TM

Scripture quotations marked NCV are taken from the New Century Version®. Copyright © 2005 by Thomas Nelson. Used by permission. All rights reserved.

What is Frazer 365?

Frazer 365 is one church's attempt to touch every member every day with the Word of God. Acts 2:46 teaches that the early church met **"day by day, attending the temple together."** While most members cannot get to our campus every day, we can still study His Word daily together in community. We believe that God works in miraculous ways when every member studies the same Scripture each day. We have also discovered that an expositional approach to the study of Scripture keeps us from skipping the difficult sections and provides us the whole counsel of God's Word.

At Frazer, we believe that the Word of God **"is living and active."** (Hebrews 4:12a)

The Bible is alive with God's truth, and it activates our spiritual growth. Proper application to our daily lives works to help us follow His will.

At Frazer, we believe that the Word of God is **"sharper than any two-edged sword, piercing to the division of soul and of spirit, of joints and of marrow."** (Hebrews 4:12b)

The Bible properly divided, penetrates our lives, and reveals the core of who we are meant to be in Christ. Scripture clearly cuts to the heart of God's purpose and plan for the life He has given us. At times, it painfully points out the sin in our lives.

At Frazer, we believe that the Word of God discerns **"the thoughts and intentions of the heart**." (Hebrews 4:12c)

The Holy Spirit speaks to us through God's Word and uncovers our thoughts and intentions. Scripture points out wrong thinking and misdirected motives and guides us back to a godly mindset, unselfish attitude, and a serving spirit.

At Frazer, we believe that: **"All Scripture is breathed out by God and profitable for teaching, for reproof, for correction, and for training in righteousness, that the man of God may be complete, equipped for every good work."** (2 Timothy 3:16-17)

At Frazer, we believe that His Word is **"a lamp to my feet."** (Psalm 119:105a)

Godly Wisdom comes from His Word. Scripture shines a light on God's will so you can see where He wants your next steps to be.

At Frazer, we believe that His Word is **"a light to my path."** (Psalm 119:105b)

As you commit to **Frazer 365**, may His Word illuminate your path as you take daily steps of faith in your journey with Him.

Joshua

LIVING THE VICTORIOUS LIFE

[6] "Be strong and courageous, for you shall cause this people to inherit the land that I swore to their fathers to give them. [7] Only be strong and very courageous, being careful to do according to all the law that Moses my servant commanded you. Do not turn from it to the right hand or to the left, that you may have good success wherever you go. [8] This Book of the Law shall not depart from your mouth, but you shall meditate on it day and night, so that you may be careful to do according to all that is written in it. For then you will make your way prosperous, and then you will have good success."

Joshua 1:6–8

Table of Contents

Joshua

Introduction

Welcome to a journey through the book of Joshua. In the Old Testament, Joshua is the first book after the five books of Moses, known as the Torah and the Pentateuch. As the sixth book of our Old Testament, it is also the first of the twelve historical books. Therefore, Joshua serves as a vital bridge between the Law of Moses and the rest of Israel's history.

Who wrote it?

The *Holman Old Testament Commentary* begins the discussion on the authorship of Joshua as follows:

> Some Bible books, like many of the prophets, are named for the author. Joshua is named for the hero or principal character. Nowhere in the book are we told that Joshua wrote it, although most scholars believe he wrote significant parts of it.[1]

Colin Peckham, in his work *Joshua: A Devotional Commentary*, gives the following discussion concerning who wrote Joshua:

> According to the Talmud (the body of Jewish law), 'Joshua wrote his own book', but there continues to be controversy over the authorship of the book. Scripture

does not identify the author and there is no conclusive evidence that Joshua wrote it. Although the human authorship may be debatable, the divine inspiration is clear. Throughout the book God has a very active role. He is the One who took the initiative for the moves made by Israel. The divine element is magnified, so the spiritual emphasis of the book must be given its proper emphasis.

Internal factors indicate that the writer lived at the time of Joshua, for example, 'until we had crossed over' (Joshua 5:1) – the 'we' gives a sense of corporate solidarity and eyewitness clarity.

Jewish tradition would probably be correct in attributing the authorship of the book to Joshua himself. We read: 'Then Joshua wrote these words in the Book of the Law of God' (Joshua 24:26).

Joshua obviously did not write all of the book, as his own death is recorded in the last chapter.[2]

The consensus among scholars is that Joshua wrote most of the book that bears his name, and that the book gives evidence of an editorial process that followed Joshua's death.

When was it written?

The *Holman Old Testament Commentary* gives the best summary answer to this question:

Great debate surrounds this question with some critical scholars suggesting a date as late as the 1200s. But evidence for an early date prevails among evangelicals. Obviously such a view (i.e., the 1200s) would preclude any contributions by Joshua who died in 1380 BC. We also know that the date of the exodus was 1446, so we surmise that most of the book was written by Joshua between 1406 and 1380, and some portions were added by other writers or editors at a later time.[3]

What was the purpose?

The purpose of Joshua can be discovered from the title of the book. In Hebrew, "Joshua" means "Yahweh saves" or "The Lord is salvation." God saved the nation of Israel through their wilderness wanderings and delivered them to the Promised Land. Therefore, the primary purpose of the book of Joshua is to detail the history of God leading His people to the land He had promised them.

David Howard's commentary adds these profound words:

Beyond its "battles," the Book of Joshua is far more interested in the land of Canaan, whose possession was the goal of the conflicts. The book begins with the detailed and careful preparations that were necessary before Israel embarked on its campaign to take this land (chaps. 1–5). These preparations had a primarily spiritual nature, emphasizing that before Israel could inherit the land, they must stand in right relationship with their God, who was graciously giving them the land.[4]

The great theologian Warren Wiersbe shares this insight into the purpose of the book of Joshua:

The word "land" is found eighty-seven times in the Book of Joshua because this book is the record of Israel's entering, conquering, and claiming the Promised

Land. God promised to give the land to Abraham, and He reaffirmed the promise to Isaac, Jacob, and their descendants. The Exodus narrative gives many reaffirmations of the promise, and these are repeated in Leviticus and Numbers.

In Moses' "farewell speech" found in Deuteronomy, he frequently mentioned the land and the nation's responsibility to possess it. The word "land" is found nearly two hundred times in Deuteronomy and the word "possess" over fifty times. Israel owned the land because of God's gracious covenant with Abraham (Genesis 12:1–5), but their enjoyment of the land depended on their faithful obedience to God.[5]

Why is it important?

Joshua: A Commentary in the Wesleyan Tradition begins its discussion of Joshua with these words:

The book of Joshua is central to the message of the Bible. It describes a crucial moment in the fulfillment of God's promise to establish his people in a land of their own. In it we see the completion of what God began in the exodus. It clarifies how God works with his people; its stories illustrate how God brings salvation. For these reasons and more, Joshua has for centuries occupied an important place within Judaism and Christianity.[6]

There are several important themes that flow through the book of Joshua. Here are just a few:

God always keeps His promises.

The word "promise" occurs fourteen times in the twenty-four chapters of Joshua.

Sincere faith leads to action.

Joshua believed in God enough to obey Him even when God gave him some challenging instructions. God called Joshua to lead his people to step into the Jordan River at flood stage and march around Jericho for seven days. Joshua's faith led to obedience to God's commands.

Purity is a prerequisite for victory.

Before several major conquests, God required his people to consecrate themselves: before Israel crossed the Jordan River, before His people defeated Jericho, and prior to the victory at Ai.

We must take possession of what God has promised.

The subtitle of our study of Joshua is "Living the Victorious Life." When God makes a promise, that does not mean that we just sit passively and wait. God has called us to work out our salvation with fear and trembling (Philippians 2:12). He has also called us to step into all that He has promised. God promised Israel a Promised Land. However, that did not mean there wouldn't be work required for Israel to possess all that God has promised. They had to battle and believe, consecrate and commit, work and worship in order to

5

live in all that God had promised. The same will be true of each of us if we seek to live the victorious Christian life that God has planned and purposed for His children.

Joshua

A Book Like No Other

Joshua's name means "Yahweh saves" or "Yahweh delivers." His name is rendered in the Old Greek traditions as the same form as Jesus' name in the New Testament. His original name was "Hoshea," which means "salvation" or "deliverance" (Numbers 13:8; Deuteronomy 32:44). Numbers 13:16 explains that Moses himself gave Hoshea his new name, "Joshua."
David M. Howard[1]

Text: Joshua 1:1-2
[1] After the death of Moses the servant of the Lord, the Lord said to Joshua the son of Nun, Moses' assistant, [2] "Moses my servant is dead. Now therefore arise, go over this Jordan, you and all this people, into the land that I am giving to them, to the people of Israel.

Thoughts:
Joshua is truly a book like no other. It is the first of its kind in several categories. Joshua is the first book in the Bible named after a person. Also, Joshua is described by many scholars as a bridge. It connects the first five books of the Old Testament, the Pentateuch, with the rest of the Old Testament. It connects the history of the nation of Israel from outside the Promised Land to living inside Canaan. This book describes how Joshua, who was born a slave in Egypt, became the conquering general in Canaan.

The book was called "Joshua" after the primary character in it. The name "Joshua" means "Yahweh is salvation." Just as the first Joshua was victorious in his conquest of Canaan, even so, the second Joshua [Jesus] was victorious in His conquest of sin.[2] A book whose main figure bears the name "Yahweh saves" should strike us as deserving close attention.

The book of Joshua begins with the death of possibly the greatest leader in the Old Testament - Moses. In the Hall of Faith, found in Hebrews 11, Moses is talked about more than any other faithful follower of Jesus. While the death of God's man brings an end to an era, it doesn't stop the plans of the Lord. Moses has an assistant, Joshua, whom God has been preparing to lead the people of Israel for approximately 80 years.

Several key events occur in Joshua's life before he takes over the role of leader. One essential aspect of Joshua's life is found in Exodus 33:7-11:

[7] Now Moses used to take the tent and pitch it outside the camp, far off from the camp, and he called it the tent of meeting. And everyone who sought the Lord would go out to the tent of meeting, which was outside the camp. [8] Whenever Moses went out to the tent, all the people would rise up, and each would stand at his tent door, and watch Moses until he had gone into the tent. [9] When Moses entered the tent, the pillar of cloud would descend and stand at the entrance of the tent, and the Lord would speak with Moses. [10] And when all the people saw the pillar of cloud standing at the entrance of the tent, all the people would rise up and worship, each at his tent door.

[11] Thus the Lord used to speak to Moses face to face, as a man speaks to his friend. When Moses turned again into the camp, his assistant Joshua the son of Nun, a young man, would not depart from the tent.

Joshua loved being in God's presence and he would not leave the tent. The word "depart" could be translated, "he refused to leave." Joshua so desired a relationship with God that he denied himself other activities so he would not miss one single moment with his Lord.

Another fundamental moment in Joshua's life is recorded in Numbers 13, when Moses sent in twelve spies to evaluate the Promised Land. Ten of the spies brought back a report of fear and said, "We can't take the land because giants live there." Only Joshua and Caleb believed that they could overcome any obstacle with God on their side. The other spies' lack of faith led to the people of Israel wandering for forty years in the wilderness. Joshua and Caleb had to wait four decades because of the lack of faith of leaders around them.

Now, Joshua's time had finally arrived. What God had promised Abraham back in Genesis 12:7 is about to be fulfilled. Joshua's patience, perseverance, and steadfast faith will finally be rewarded.

Before we get too far into the study of this great book, we need to clarify some confusion. Many of our old hymns refer to Canaan in language that compares the Promised Land to Heaven. In one hymn, people sing, "And there will be no sorrow there, in that tomorrow, we will be there by and by. Milk and honey flowing there is where I'm going, Canaanland is just in sight." Another song states, "To Canaan's land I'm on my way, where the soul never dies." Notice how Max Lucado clears up this misconception.

Canaan symbolizes the victory we can have today . . . Canaan is not a metaphor for heaven. The idea is beautiful, but the symbolism doesn't work. Heaven will have no enemies; Canaan had at least seven enemy nations. Heaven will have no battles. Joshua and his men fought at least thirty-one (Joshua 12:9–24). Heaven will be free of stumbles and struggle. Joshua's men weren't. They stumbled and struggled, but their victories far outnumbered their defeats.

Canaan, then, does not represent the life to come. Canaan represents the life we can have now!

God invites us to enter Canaan. There is only one condition. We must turn our backs on the wilderness.[3]

Canaan is a picture of the victorious Christian life. The Promised Land depicts God's best for His children. There will be battles to face and giants to fight, but spiritual victories await those who follow Him wholeheartedly.

As we start this journey through the book of Joshua, don't settle for anything less than God's best for you. The journey won't be easy, but the rewards will be worth the fight.

Questions:

1. As you start this study of Joshua, are you wandering in a spiritual wilderness or are you living a victorious Christian life? Explain your answer.

2. God called His people out of slavery so that He could take them into victory. What specifically are you being called out from?

3. What distracts you from being in His presence? What will it take for you to be like Joshua and worship God fully and trust Him completely?

Day Two

Joshua
─────────

Promises with Responsibilities

*We show that we really believe God's promises
only when we begin to obey His commands.*
David Jackman[1]

Text: Joshua 1:3-5

[3] Every place that the sole of your foot will tread upon
I have given to you, just as I promised to Moses. [4] From the
wilderness and this Lebanon as far as the great river, the
river Euphrates, all the land of the Hittites to the Great Sea
toward the going down of the sun shall be your territory. [5] No
man shall be able to stand before you all the days of your life.
Just as I was with Moses, so I will be with you. I will not leave
you or forsake you.

Thoughts:

As we study Joshua together, you will discover that this
book is filled with spiritual applications to our present journey
with Jesus. Max Lucado adds the following insight:

The Promised Land was the third stop on the
Hebrews' iconic itinerary. Their pilgrimage began in
Egypt, continued through the wilderness, and concluded
in Canaan. Each land represents a different condition of
life. Geography is theology. In Egypt, the Hebrews were
enslaved to Pharaoh. In the wilderness, they were free
from Pharaoh but still enslaved to fear. They refused to

enter the Promised Land and languished in the desert. Only in Canaan did they discover victory. Egypt, the wilderness, and Canaan: Slaves to Pharaoh, slaves to fear, and, finally, people of the promise.[2]

Our Christian journey is similar. God sets Christians free from sin's penalty and gives us victory over sin's power. However, many people wander in the wilderness of defeat because they don't take responsibility to live in the victory that God has for them.

Joshua 1:3-5 outlines God's promise to the nation of Israel, but verse 3 explains that they must step foot on the land in order to inherit it. Scholars have estimated the total amount of land God promised was 300,000 square miles, encompassing modern-day Israel, Jordan, and Iraq. At the height of their success during the days of David and Solomon, the Israelites controlled 30,000 square miles – only a tenth of all that God had promised them!

David Jackman, in his commentary on Joshua, addresses this issue:

> If Joshua's forward advance was dependent on believing God's promises in detail, how is it that so much of this promise was never fulfilled? Preachers need to deal with such objections and questions, or they will certainly undermine the faith of their hearers. There seem to be two important considerations to bring out. The first is that the actualization of what is promised is dependent on the wholehearted obedience of God's people. The sadness of the book is that the conquest was far from complete, that compromise and comfort took over, and that many of the inhabitants of the land were never dislodged.

The same unbelief and lack of faith that precluded their entry to the land forty years earlier surfaced in the next generation in an unwillingness to push forward with the complete conquest after the initial gains had been secured. "They were unable to enter because of unbelief" (Hebrews 3:19)—that is said of the exodus generation, but by extension, exactly the same weakness was revealed in their descendants.[3]

When Israel stepped out in faith, they experienced the victory God had promised. When they compromised and settled for less, they missed God's best.

God specifically told Israel that the journey to occupy the Promised Land would be a difficult process. In Exodus 23:29-30, God said:

> [29] I will not drive them out from before you in one year, lest the land become desolate and the wild beasts multiply against you. [30] Little by little I will drive them out from before you, until you have increased and possess the land.

Since it would be an ongoing process, they would have to trust God every step of the way. They would need His power and wisdom for their daily victories, so that they could ultimately possess all God had promised them.

Our Christian life is synonymous with Israel's journey. God has promised us victory. He has provided His Word and the Holy Spirit to guide us to spiritual success. However, we must trust Him fully and serve Him faithfully to experience all that He has promised. God forbid that we live with only a tenth of the victory of all that He has waiting for us.

Questions:

1. Read the last part of Joshua 1:5 carefully: "Just as I was with Moses, so I will be with you. I will not leave you or forsake you." What does it mean for you to take God's promises for your life seriously? Give some examples.

2. Why do you think the Israelites struggled for generations to believe God's promise to them that He would give them the land of Canaan?

3. What is your response to David Jackman's quote that begins today's devotion?

> "We show that we really believe God's promises only when we begin to obey His commands."

Day Three

Joshua

Be Strong and Courageous

God has brought courage to the hearts of those who love Him. The Bible is crowded with assurances of God's help and comfort in every kind of trouble which might cause fears to arise in the human heart. Today the Christian can come to the Scriptures with full assurance that God is going to deliver the person who puts his trust and confidence in God.
Billy Graham[1]

Text: Joshua 1:6-7

[6] Be strong and courageous, for you shall cause this people to inherit the land that I swore to their fathers to give them.

[7] Only be strong and very courageous, being careful to do according to all the law that Moses my servant commanded you. Do not turn from it to the right hand or to the left, that you may have good success wherever you go.

Thoughts:

"Be Strong and courageous" was the ongoing command from God to the nation of Israel. This phrase is found eleven times in the Old Testament. Five of those eleven occurrences are found in the book of Joshua. Four of the five occasions are found in the first chapter of Joshua.

In the language of the Old Testament, this phrase is a double imperative. In Hebrew, "be strong" is "chazak." This word means "to become strong and be resolute in order to prevail. "Be courageous" is "ematz." "Ematz" means "to be alert, brave, and determined." God commanded His people to be strong and to have courage. Brian Harbour explains this command as follows:

> One would suspect that the constant repetition of this phrase was because Joshua and the Israelites had every reason to be timid and fearful. And they did. They had a river to cross. They had a city (Jericho) to defeat. They had a land to possess. They had a right to be timid and fearful.
> We often think courage means the absence of fear. It would be more realistic to say courage and fear are usually intermingled. Courage does not mean the absence of fear. Courage means to act despite the presence of fear.[2]

Joshua 1:7 instructed Joshua how he could remain obedient to God's command to be strong and courageous.

His strength to obey would come from "being careful to do according to all the law that Moses my servant commanded" them. In other words, obeying God's Word would help him to stay strong and courageous.

The last part of verse 7 was another command from God: "Do not turn from it to the right hand or the left, that you may have good success wherever you go." God makes Himself known through His Word. Joshua would know the God of the Word personally by his commitment to obeying the Word of God faithfully. If he didn't waiver in his obedience, he wouldn't fluctuate between victories and defeats. A constant obedience to God's Word would lead to a consistent victory through His power.

God specifically said this law to be obeyed was what Moses commanded. Francis Schaeffer gave a profound lesson here:

Joshua knew Moses, the writer of the Pentateuch, personally. Joshua knew his strengths and weaknesses as a man; he knew that Moses was a sinner, that Moses made mistakes, and that Moses was just a man. Nonetheless, immediately after Moses's death, Joshua accepted the Pentateuch as more than the writing of Moses. He accepted it as the writing of God. Two or three hundred years were not required for the book to become sacred. As far as Joshua was concerned the Pentateuch was the canon, and the canon was the Word of God. The biblical view of the growth and acceptance of the canon is as simple as this: When it was given, God's people understood what it was. Right away it had authority.[3]

Alan Carr applied God's command to Joshua to our lives today:

Joshua would need great courage to face the enemies of Israel and to lead the people to victory in the promised land. God's challenge to Joshua is for him to stand!

There is just as great a need for people to stand for the Lord now as there was in the days of Joshua! All around us, Christians are falling by the wayside. What we need is for God's children to be moved in the depths of their souls to stand up, renew their commitments to the Lord, and say, "By God's help, I'll stand and not fall all the days of my life!" We need people today who will take the lead in their churches and make their stand for the Lord. It is high time that the church stopped letting herself be a doormat for the world and the devil. It is time we stood up and made our stand with the people of God and heeded God's call to be brave and strong in these days.[4]

Questions:

1. In what ways are you exercising courage and strength in your life as a Christian?

2. How does obeying His Word give you the courage and strength to stand for Christ?

3. How do the following Scriptures relate to today's Scripture?

1 Corinthians 15:58 (ESV)

Therefore, my beloved brothers, be steadfast, immovable, always abounding in the work of the Lord, knowing that in the Lord your labor is not in vain.

Romans 13:11–14 (ESV)

[11] Besides this you know the time, that the hour has come for you to wake from sleep. For salvation is nearer to us now than when we first believed. [12] The night is far gone; the day is at hand. So then let us cast off the works of darkness and put on the armor of light. [13] Let us walk properly as in the daytime, not in orgies and drunkenness, not in sexual immorality and sensuality, not in quarreling and jealousy.

[14] But put on the Lord Jesus Christ, and make no provision for the flesh, to gratify its desires.

Day Four

Joshua

His Word and His Presence

The word of God reveals God's will for His people,
and His presence enables them to achieve His purpose.
Kenneth Matthews [1]

Text: Joshua 1:8-9

[8] This Book of the Law shall not depart from your mouth, but you shall meditate on it day and night, so that you may be careful to do according to all that is written in it. For then you will make your way prosperous, and then you will have good success. [9] Have I not commanded you? Be strong and courageous. Do not be frightened, and do not be dismayed, for the Lord your God is with you wherever you go."

Thoughts:

God centered His command to be strong and courageous around a commitment to the "Book of the Law." Joshua 1:8 gives a threefold approach to God's Word. First, this book "shall not depart from your mouth." In other words, we should keep speaking God's truth from His Word. You cannot regularly speak God's Word from your mouth if you don't constantly have God's Word in your heart. Thus, the next statement is ". . . you shall meditate on it day and night." The word for "meditate" means "to groan or utter." When you meditate on God's Word, you say it repeatedly in your mind and contemplate it deeply in your heart. If you keep your mind fixed on His Word and constantly speak His truths to your heart, then you will be careful to obey it. So, the third step is to obey God's Word with your life. The process is as follows: Speak God's Word consistently because you meditate on it regularly, and you will obey it faithfully. When this happens, God says that you will prosper spiritually and have good success in your Christian life.

Max Lucado stresses how essential God's Word is to every believer:

> Like you and me, Joshua had a Bible. His Bible had five books—Genesis, Exodus, Leviticus, Numbers, and at least portions of Deuteronomy—which were carried alongside the ark of the covenant. But it wasn't enough for Joshua to possess the Scriptures; God wanted the Scriptures to possess Joshua. "This Book of the Law shall not depart from your mouth" (v. 8).
>
> This was God's command to the commander of Israel. Though he was the unquestioned five-star general of the army, Joshua was subject to God's law. God did not tell him to create law or invent statutes but to be regulated by what was "written."
>
> God didn't command Joshua to seek a spiritual experience, pursue a personal revelation, or long for goosebumps-giving emotion. God's Word to him is His Word to us: open the Bible.
>
> The Bible is the most important tool in our spiritual growth. We can say this with confidence because of the good work of Greg Hawkins and Cally Parkinson. In the research for their book *Move*, they set out to find the key factors for spiritual growth. They asked the same question that we are asking: How do we move out of the wilderness into Canaan? Out of weak faith into life-giving faith?
>
> Their study was conducted by an independent market research firm. The secular company had no

agenda other than to earn their fees by accurate analysis. They surveyed people in a thousand churches. And what they discovered raised the eyebrows of at least a thousand pastors.

Nothing has a greater impact on spiritual growth than reflection on Scripture. If churches could do only one thing to help people at all levels of spiritual maturity grow in their relationship with Christ, their choice is clear. They would inspire, encourage, and equip their people to read the Bible.

The key to spiritual growth is not increased church attendance or involvement in spiritual activities. People don't grow in Christ because they are busy at church. They grow in Christ when they read and trust their Bibles.[2]

In verse 9, God reminded Joshua of His presence with the statement, "God is with you wherever you go." God declared to him that he didn't have to walk this journey alone.

We find our ability to be strong and courageous in His Word and His presence. God's presence abides with those who obey His Word. Dale Ralph Davis adds the following:

Joshua is not told to grit his teeth and build up his courage on his own; he is to be strong only because Yahweh is with him.[3]

Yes, we have His promise, and we have the power of His Word, but we also have Him! He is with us every step of the way! You don't have to face your giants alone. You don't have to get to the Promised Land by yourself. You don't have to conquer your addictions in a solo journey. God is with you. His name is Immanuel. You can be strong and courageous because He is right there!

Questions:

1. In what ways are you speaking God's Word consistently?

> Here are a few suggestions:
> - Reciting Scripture aloud.
> - Listening to Scripture on an app.

2. In what ways are you meditating on God's Word regularly?

> Here are a few suggestions:
> - Reading the same passage of Scripture over a certain time.
> - Memorizing a Scripture.
> - Journaling your thoughts about a passage of Scripture.

3. Are you a doer of God's Word? If so, in what ways?

4. How does knowing God is there, give you the strength and courage to obey His Word?

Day Five

Joshua

Preparation Precedes Victory

It does not require great learning to be a Christian
convinced of the truth of the Bible.
It requires only an honest heart
and a willingness to obey God.
Albert Barnes[1]

Text: Joshua 1:10-11

[10] And Joshua commanded the officers of the people, [11] "Pass through the midst of the camp and command the people, 'Prepare your provisions, for within three days you are to pass over this Jordan to go in to take possession of the land that the Lord your God is giving you to possess.'"

Thoughts:

After God issued His challenge to Joshua, Joshua commanded his leaders. When God prepares His spiritual leader, those under that person's leadership must also be prepared. It requires a great trust in your spiritual leaders to act upon what they say God told them to do. It also takes a willingness to surrender and submit.

To possess all that God has for us, each part of God's family must be spiritually prepared to move when God says move and fight when God says fight. Preparation doesn't follow success. Success follows preparation.

Robert Smith Jr. describes the path of leadership in verses 10-11 as follows:

The trajectory is from God to people and not from people to people. Even today, God prepares his leader just as he had prepared Joshua to lead, and then he leads his leader to lead leaders. God is a God of order. God's ways begin with sovereignty and descend to humanity. When I was a little boy, I would hear the elders say, "God sits high, and he looks low." In today's society, we are familiar with the order that begins with us and ends with us. Joshua takes the words he has heard from God in verse 10 and gives the orders to the officers of the people; there is no disconnect between what he has heard God say and what he says to the officers.

The officers in turn were to communicate the orders to the people without modification. The people did not resist God's plan. This is God's way of leadership for the church today.[2]

Joshua was able to lead God's people because he himself spent forty years learning under a great leader – Moses. He obeyed the Word of the Lord that came to Moses, submitting to his leadership and witnessing God do amazing miracles through him. Joshua was probably in his forties when he watched the Red Sea open before him and he walked across on dry ground. This was essential spiritual preparation. Numbers 27:18 states that Moses knew the Spirit of God was on Joshua. By the time Joshua became the leader, he fully believed that nothing was impossible with God. Therefore, he did not question crossing the Jordan, even during its flood stage, when the river would have been at its deepest and most dangerous to cross.

Joshua sent word to every person through his leaders to prepare their provisions. In three days, they were going to cross into the Promised Land, a land flowing with milk and honey. A look back to Exodus 16:35 will provide some clarity at this point:

> The people of Israel ate the manna forty years, till they came to a habitable land. They ate the manna till they came to the border of the land of Canaan.

We see that God provided manna for His people throughout their wilderness wanderings, but this would cease once they crossed the river. Instead of simply eating the miraculous manna each day, the people would have to gather and prepare their own food, using the Promised Land's abundant resources. The resources ultimately came from God, but the people were responsible for working in this new land of blessing.

We also are called to work out what God provides. Paul describes this concept to the church at Philippi in Philippians 2:12:

> Therefore, my beloved, as you have always obeyed, so now, not only as in my presence but much more in my absence, work out your own salvation with fear and trembling . . .

What God works in, we are to work out. God saves us from our sins by His grace and not by our works. But after we are saved, we have a responsibility to discipline ourselves to live in the fullness of all that God has saved us for. As we have previously learned, God has brought us out so that He can bring us in. God saved us from our sins so that He can reconcile us back into a right relationship with Himself. We must continue to prepare ourselves spiritually for all that God has for our future in Him. Living in spiritual victory doesn't come without constantly preparing ourselves for what lies ahead. Never forget: preparation precedes victory.

Questions:

1. Do you trust your spiritual leaders enough to help carry out what God tells them to do? How does your submission involve spiritual preparation?

2. If you are a spiritual leader to a certain group of people, how is your spiritual preparation connected to your great responsibility to hear God's voice?

3. How are you preparing yourself spiritually for all that God has in store for your life?

Day Six

Joshua

Don't Settle for Less

The key to Christian living is a thirst and hunger for God.
One of the main reasons people do not understand or
experience the sovereignty of grace and the way it works
through the awakening of sovereign joy is that their hunger
and thirst for God is so small.
John Piper[1]

Text: Joshua 1:12-15
¹² And to the Reubenites, the Gadites, and the half-tribe of Manasseh Joshua said, ¹³ "Remember the word that Moses the servant of the Lord commanded you, saying, 'The Lord your God is providing you a place of rest and will give you this land.' ¹⁴ Your wives, your little ones, and your livestock shall remain in the land that Moses gave you beyond the Jordan, but all the men of valor among you shall pass over armed before your brothers and shall help them, ¹⁵ until the Lord gives rest to your brothers as he has to you, and they also take possession of the land that the Lord your God is giving them. Then you shall return to the land of your possession and shall possess it, the land that Moses the servant of the Lord gave you beyond the Jordan toward the sunrise."

Thoughts:
In this section of Scripture, Joshua spoke to the tribes of Reuben, Gad, and the half-tribe of Manasseh. Numbers 32

explains how these tribes requested to settle just outside the Promised Land:

> ¹ Now the people of Reuben and the people of Gad had a very great number of livestock. And they saw the land of Jazer and the land of Gilead, and behold, the place was a place for livestock. ² So the people of Gad and the people of Reuben came and said to Moses and to Eleazar the priest and to the chiefs of the congregation, . . . ⁴ "the land that the Lord struck down before the congregation of Israel, is a land for livestock, and your servants have livestock." ⁵ And they said, "If we have found favor in your sight, let this land be given to your servants for a possession. Do not take us across the Jordan."

Notice the reason for their request. The land looked profitable in their eyes, so they thought they needed it. However, this land that looked prosperous was also extremely dangerous. Many years later, the Assyrian army attacked the nation of Israel from the east. Because these two-and-a-half tribes had settled east and just outside of the Promised Land, they were the first tribes taken into captivity. These tribes also never returned to their land.

Alan Carr applies the truth of this text in the following commentary:

> There is a very powerful lesson for us in these verses. We have literal legions of Christians who are just like these 2½ tribes. They are more concerned about making a living than they are about making a life! The primary thing that motivates them is getting ahead in life. In other words, they are materially minded instead of spiritually minded! These people represent those Christians I

would call "borderline Christians". These are people who have trusted Jesus for salvation, but that is about as far as they are willing to go. They will come when they want to, tithe when they feel like they can afford to, and fight a battle now and again; but most often, they are seen just playing around the edges, refusing to put God first in their lives. By the way, it is this type of Christian who is usually the first to fall in times of attack and temptation! People who live like this can say anything they want to, but the truth is obvious: they have other gods in their lives to whom they have sold their souls! If you really love God, then how about deciding to cross on over today? Make the decision to leave behind anything that is holding you back from serving God like you should. You can rationalize it all you want to, but the truth still remains, many are choosing gold, and other worldly things, over God! If you refuse to line up with the will of God for your life, then you can be assured of the fact that one day, you will fall.[2]

Questions:

1. The tribes discussed in today's devotional still had to fight for victory, but they settled for less than God's best and it would later cost them dearly. In what ways are you tempted to settle for something you think is good that could cost you God's best?

2. What are your thoughts on Alan Carr's description of these tribes as "borderline Christians" who are living on the edges?

3. Even after these tribes experienced victory in the Promised Land, they still returned and settled for land just outside of what God had provided. How do you think people can experience God's victory in their lives and then revert back to a life of defeat?

4. After you consider your thoughts about why other people choose to stay outside God's best, reflect on why you struggle with stepping into all that God has waiting for you spiritually.

Joshua

Selective Memory vs. Surrendered Lives

Wherever you are, be all there. Live to the hilt
every situation you believe to be the will of God.
Jim Elliot[1]

Text: Joshua 1:16-18

[16] And they answered Joshua, "All that you have commanded us we will do, and wherever you send us we will go. [17] Just as we obeyed Moses in all things, so we will obey you. Only may the Lord your God be with you, as he was with Moses!

[18] Whoever rebels against your commandment and disobeys your words, whatever you command him, shall be put to death. Only be strong and courageous."

Thoughts:

In Joshua 1:16, the two-and-a-half tribes that settled east of the Promised Land told Joshua, "All that you have commanded us we will do." This is exactly what their ancestors had said to Moses in Exodus 19:8: "All the people answered together and said, "All that the Lord has spoken we will do." In the second half of Joshua 1:16, they declare even deeper allegiance: ". . . and wherever you send us we will go."

The two-and-a-half tribes then make a still more audacious statement in verse 17. "Just as we obeyed Moses in all things, so we will obey you." This generation that would inherit the Promised Land watched a generation before them continually disobey God's leadership. If you follow the Israelites after they leave Mount Sinai, you will see the previous generation rebelled against Moses seven times across eleven chapters of Numbers. (See Numbers 11-21.) They continually complained and spoke against Moses. This wasn't just a few critical people. The whole nation complained. Numbers 16:41 states, ". . . all the congregation of the people of Israel grumbled against Moses and against Aaron. . ." They did not fully obey Moses, and these two-and-a-half tribes will not fully obey Joshua either."

They continue to voice their commitment in verse 18: "Whoever rebels against your commandment and disobeys your words, whatever you command him, shall be put to death." Their statement would be fulfilled just a few chapters later in Joshua 8 when Israel is defeated at Ai. As we will see in our study, Achan and his entire family will be stoned in the Valley of Trouble because Achan disobeyed God's commands.

When we consider our own tendencies, we see that – just like the disobedient tribes – the problem isn't that we don't know what to do--it's that we don't do it. Sometimes we have selective memory when it comes to our faith journey. More than vocal commitments, we need surrendered lives. If we would only be strong and courageous and follow through on what we say we will do, we would live with all that God has promised us.

Disobedience and disunity have done irrevocable harm to God's people. Constant arguments and disputes have not only destroyed our witness, they have also caused us to miss many spiritual victories that God had planned for us in Promised Land living. *The Preacher's Commentary Series* on Joshua has a great illustration of the unity needed by God's people to serve one another in love:

The story is told of a man who died and stepped into the presence of Saint Peter. He asked if he could take a look at both heaven and hell. Saint Peter showed him a large banquet room of people eating magnificently prepared food. Then Peter took him to another large banquet room. Again, the man saw people eating magnificently prepared food. Somewhat confused, he asked Saint Peter, "Which of these rooms is heaven? Which is hell? They look the same to me."

Saint Peter said, "Let's go back and look more carefully at the persons in each of these rooms." The man did look and then noted that the only eating utensil assigned to each person in the two rooms was a long, sharp sword. In one room, the people were selfishly stabbing at their food and slashing their faces and bodies in their endeavor to feed themselves. In the other room, the people had learned to pierce the food with the sword and then to ever so tenderly and sensitively feed each other.

Hell was the room filled with people so determined to do things their way that it was ending up a place of mangled, bloody bodies. Heaven was the room of unity, love, and joy.

A people mobilized for action involves the interaction of qualified leadership and unselfish persons with unified, common goals.[2]

Questions:

1. How have you seen the consequences of the disobedience of God's people? What personally have you missed out on because of disunity and rebellion against God and His leadership?

2. Name one time that you expressed strong commitment to carrying out God's will for your life, and then fell short of living out that commitment.

3. Do you think the two-and-a-half tribes intended to keep the commitment expressed in today's verses? Why or why not?

Day Eight

Joshua

The God of Grace and Mercy

The first story in Joshua is a story of God's mercy
rather than of His wrath.
James Montgomery Boice[1]

Text: Joshua 2:1
   [1]And Joshua the son of Nun sent two men secretly from Shittim as spies, saying, "Go, view the land, especially Jericho." And they went and came into the house of a prostitute whose name was Rahab and lodged there.

Thoughts:
   The first chapter of Joshua ends with Israel preparing to cross the Jordan and take the Promised Land. The last few verses ensure that the two-and-a-half tribes that will settle east of Canaan will assist them in the conquest. One would think that the first words in the next chapter would be Israel conquering cities and destroying nations. While that will come later, God has eyes on the salvation of a prostitute who lives in Jericho. Her name is Rahab. While God will eventually destroy the entire city, He saved Rahab's family because of her faith and His grace and mercy.
   While many people have trouble understanding a God who would destroy entire nations for wickedness, we need to remember that first and foremost, God's grace is displayed to anyone who repents and trusts in Him. Kenneth Matthews declares, "Although Rahab is a Canaanite and a prostitute,

her deliverance shows that God's grace extends to any person who will confess Him.[2] James, the half-brother of Jesus, understood this when he wrote in James 2:13, "Mercy triumphs over judgment." The Apostle Paul knew that "there is no condemnation for those who are in Christ Jesus." (See Romans 8:1).

First and foremost, we have a God who saves. Remember what Joshua's name means" "Yahweh is savior." And barely two chapters into a book named "Yahweh is savior," we see God saving the life of a prostitute named Rahab.

Max Lucado writes it beautifully:

> Her résumé needn't mention her profession. Yet in five of the eight appearances of her name in Scripture, she is presented as a "harlot." Five! Wouldn't one suffice? And couldn't that one reference be nuanced in a euphemism such as "Rahab, the best *hostess* in Jericho" or "Rahab, who made everyone feel welcome"? It's bad enough that the name Rahab sounds like "rehab." Disguise her career choice. Veil it. Mask it. Put a little concealer on this biblical blemish. Drop the reference to the brothel, please.
>
> But the Bible doesn't. Just the opposite. It points a neon sign at it. It's even attached to her name in the book of Hebrews Hall of Fame. The list includes Abel, Noah, Abraham, Isaac, Jacob, Joseph, Moses . . . and then, all of a sudden, "the harlot Rahab" (11:31). No asterisk, no footnote, no apology. Her history of harlotry is part of her testimony.[3]

When God displays His mercy and grace, it testifies to His power to save and demonstrates His love for the lost.

Our salvation is why Jesus was sent from Heaven to Earth. It was all part of God's plan. Luke 19:10 proclaims, "For the Son of Man came to seek and to save the lost." God sought out Rahab to save her and her entire family. His plan involved two spies and a scarlet cord. God is still seeking out the lost. His plan includes His only Son and a blood-stained cross!

God's plan has many facets. His plan is so perfect, it projects far into the future. Joshua Chapter 2 records the plan to save Rahab. Nobody but God knew at this point in time that Jesus' family tree would include this Canaanite prostitute from Jericho. We read these words in Matthew 1:5: ". . . and Salmon the father of Boaz by Rahab . . ." Only God could save a prostitute from an enemy nation and plan the birth of His Son through her lineage. He is the God of mercy and grace. Warren Wiersbe says:

> The Bible associates Rahab with the Messiah! When you read the genealogy of the Lord Jesus Christ in Matthew 1, you find Rahab's name listed there (vs. 5), along with Jacob, David, and the other famous people in the messianic line. She has certainly come a long way from being a pagan prostitute to being an ancestress of the Messiah! "But where sin abounded, grace did much more abound." (Romans 5:20).[4]

Just as God had a plan for saving Rahab, God has a salvation plan for your life too. His plan for you has eternal projections. He wants to save you from your sins and give you the privilege of living in spiritual victory. You could call that Promised Land living.

Questions:

1. In what ways have you seen God's mercy and grace displayed in your own life?

2. What does it say about God that He saves whosoever puts their trust in Him?

3. God cares about every individual soul. He must punish sin because He is holy and just, but He has a plan to save. His "mercy triumphs over judgment." (See James 2:13.) However, His triumph works through your trust. Faith opens the door for you to receive His forgiveness and salvation. Have you received His salvation? If so, in what ways are you growing spiritually and living in victory? If you haven't trusted in Jesus for salvation, why not?

Day Nine

Joshua

Focus on the God who Saves and Your Faith

When you throw mud at someone,
you're the one who is losing ground.
Anonymous[1]

Text: Joshua 2:2-7

² And it was told to the king of Jericho, "Behold, men of Israel have come here tonight to search out the land." ³ Then the king of Jericho sent to Rahab, saying, "Bring out the men who have come to you, who entered your house, for they have come to search out all the land." ⁴ But the woman had taken the two men and hidden them. And she said, "True, the men came to me, but I did not know where they were from. ⁵ And when the gate was about to be closed at dark, the men went out. I do not know where the men went. Pursue them quickly, for you will overtake them." ⁶ But she had brought them up to the roof and hid them with the stalks of flax that she had laid in order on the roof. ⁷ So the men pursued after them on the way to the Jordan as far as the fords. And the gate was shut as soon as the pursuers had gone out.

Thoughts:

Critics can ask negative questions and give dangerous advice. One misguided question that has been asked about Joshua 2 is: "Did Joshua lack faith by sending spies into the Promised Land?" We might ask: "If Joshua had already seen the Promised Land some forty years earlier, why would he need to scout it out again? If he had complete faith in God, why not just cross over and take the land?" The *Holman Old Testament Commentary* gives a great response to these questions:

> The use of the spies was not a lack of faith but rather a demonstration that true faith is active faith. Like Joshua, we must use common sense and caution as we march through our Christian lives.[2]

Another question people have about this passage revolves around Rahab's lie. Some misdirected students of God's Word try to excavate from these verses a justification to lie when necessary. The Bible clearly calls lying a sin. Leviticus 19:11 reads, "You shall not steal; you shall not deal falsely; you shall not lie to one another." When we focus on Rahab's lie, we miss the facts about her faith. Commentator Dale Ralph Davis offers great counsel here:

> It is tragic when people snag their pants on the nail of Rahab's lie, quibble endlessly about the matter, and never get around to hearing Rahab's *truth*.[3]

Our focus in this Scripture should be on Rahab's faith and God's salvation. Scholars of God's Word can get our focus back on track:

> Clearly, Rahab, not the spies, is the star here—and the only fully human character, too. Aside from Joshua, she is the only one known by name.[4]

> This chapter centers not on the spies or Joshua himself but on Rahab the prostitute. She demonstrates for us the wisdom and value of choosing faith and acting upon that choice. Her reward was enormous.[5]

Present behind the scenes, Yahweh's providential work through Rahab proves Him to be a gracious and hands-on divine warrior.[6]

We must be careful in our study of Scripture not to over-emphasize the faults of others and overlook the applications for the goodness of God. If we are not careful, we will miss God's best by rationalizing our sins and questioning what God has already clearly answered in His Word. Rather than seek to justify what we know the Bible clearly defines as sin; let's focus on the God who saves us and our daily spiritual growth. Let's shut the gate to negativity and focus on living in God's perfect will. May we close the door on a critical spirit and open the door to all that God has for us in the future!

Questions:

1. In what ways do we tend to focus on the sins and shortcomings of those whom God has saved?

2. What needs to change in your life so that you can focus more on the goodness of God's salvation and the truth of His Word?

3. Rahab went to extreme measures, even risking her life to hide the two spies. By doing so, she found salvation for herself and her family. What are you risking for Jesus? In what ways does your faith need to grow to extreme measures?

Day Ten

Joshua

"The Lord Your God, He is God."

Rahab showed more faith in the Lord than the ten spies had exhibited forty years before, when she said, "I know that the Lord has given you the land." (Joshua 2:9). Her faith was based on facts, not just feelings; for she had heard of the miracles God had performed, starting with the opening up of the Red Sea at the Exodus. "So then faith comes by hearing, and hearing by the Word of God." (Romans 10:17).
Warren Wiersbe[1]

Text: Joshua 2:8-11
⁸ Before the men lay down, she came up to them on the roof ⁹ and said to the men, "I know that the Lord has given you the land, and that the fear of you has fallen upon us, and that all the inhabitants of the land melt away before you.

¹⁰ For we have heard how the Lord dried up the water of the Red Sea before you when you came out of Egypt, and what you did to the two kings of the Amorites who were beyond the Jordan, to Sihon and Og, whom you devoted to destruction. ¹¹ And as soon as we heard it, our hearts melted, and there was no spirit left in any man because of you, for the Lord your God, he is God in the heavens above and on the earth beneath.

Thoughts:
Rahab has a remarkable conversation with the two spies on the roof of her house. She had heard of the greatness of God, and great fear had fallen on her heart. Twice Rahab uses the word

46

"melted." These are two different words in the Hebrew language. In verse 9, she stated, ". . . all the inhabitants of the land melt away before you." This word for melt means "to dissolve away" or "cause to lose heart." In verse 11, Rahab said, ". . . our hearts melted . . ." This Old Testament word means "to melt away as worthless" and "to completely lose heart." It can also mean "to liquefy." God had dissolved the Canaanites' callous hearts, and they were losing any hopes to defeat Him.

Both of these statements about melting away in fear are tied to what Rahab heard. At some point in the past, she had heard about the God of Israel. Joshua 2:10 reveals that she had specifically heard about the Red Sea incident and the defeat of the two kings of the Amorites, Sihon and Og. What she heard produced a change in her heart. The testimony of God's power had softened her heart. The stories of God's miracles had brought a reverent fear of God to her heart. Rahab had thought often about who God was and all that He had done.

Scripture teaches us that salvation is always preceded by hearing. Romans 10:17 says, "So faith comes from hearing, and hearing through the Word of Christ." Every Christian was saved because someone somewhere told them about the Lord. And like Rahab, God's Word softens our hearts.

With a softened heart, Rahab confesses a faith in God. Verse 11 contains Rahab's marvelous statement about God. ". . . for the Lord your God, He is God in the heavens above and on the earth beneath." This is an incredible announcement on any level, but especially from a Canaanite. As a Canaanite, Rahab would have worshiped false idols such as Baal and Asherah. Baal was known as the god of the Canaanites, yet Rahab announced that the God of Israel is the God of all Heaven and Earth. Her confession is her way of saying, "While there have been many false gods in my life, there is only one true God – and He is the God of Israel!" She had heard about the God of Israel, and now she is confessing Him to be the Lord of all.

David Howard, in the *New American Commentary*, adds the following comments:

> "Yahweh" was the true God's personal name, just as "Baal" or "Asherah," "Marduk," or "Ishtar" were the personal names of Canaanite and Babylonian gods, respectively. Thus, when Rahab stated that "Yahweh your God is God," she was stating that Baal, Asherah, and the rest were not true gods.
>
> Rahab's words become even more significant when we realize that the last part of her affirmation—the phrase "in the heavens above and the earth below"—is found only three times prior to this, all in contexts that affirm God's exclusive claims to sovereignty.[2]

Warren Wiersbe reaffirms this thought:

> Rahab's conversion was truly an act of God's grace. Like all the citizens of Canaan, Rahab was under condemnation and destined to die. God commanded the Jews to "utterly destroy them" and show them no mercy (Deuteronomy 7:1–3). Rahab was a Gentile, outside the covenant mercies shown to Israel (Ephesians 2:11–13). She didn't deserve to be saved, but God had mercy on her. If ever a sinner experienced Ephesians 2:1–10, it was Rahab![3]

Questions:

1. How is Rahab's confession connected to her reverent fear of God?

2. When people hear about your faith and witness your God, do they say, "The Lord your God, He is God"? How can your life be a greater testimony of God's power and grace?

3. In what ways is the response to God's power in Elijah's life, seen in the Scripture below, similar to Rahab's response?

1 Kings 18:38-39 (ESV)
   [38] Then the fire of the Lord fell and consumed the burnt offering and the wood and the stones and the dust, and licked up the water that was in the trench. [39] And when all the people saw it, they fell on their faces and said, "The Lord, He is God; the Lord, He is God."

Day Eleven

Joshua

Covenant Commitment

Here's the trade: Rahab saves the messengers while the men of Jericho are in control, and the messengers are to save Rahab later once the Israelites are in control.
Pekka M. Pitkänen [1]

Text: Joshua 2:12-14

[12] Now then, please swear to me by the Lord that, as I have dealt kindly with you, you also will deal kindly with my father's house, and give me a sure sign [13] that you will save alive my father and mother, my brothers and sisters, and all who belong to them, and deliver our lives from death." [14] And the men said to her, "Our life for yours even to death! If you do not tell this business of ours, then when the Lord gives us the land we will deal kindly and faithfully with you."

Thoughts:

We read yesterday that Rahab and the Canaanites greatly fear the Lord. David Jackman, in his commentary on Joshua, writes:

> The truth of who God is and what He has done for His people has already penetrated Jericho, and when the word of God gets into enemy territory, only two reactions are possible. Either there is faith in the greatness of the Lord and a casting of oneself entirely on His mercy (vs. 12, 13), or there is fear, which determines to resist

God's supremacy, challenge His will, and continue to fight against His purposes. . . Once the uniqueness of His sovereign authority and power over the whole of creation is realized, the reaction can only be submission or resistance. In the face of God's purposes, neutrality is impossible.[2]

There is no neutral ground when it comes to following God.

Serving God fully requires keeping our word faithfully. In fact, God told His people through His servant Moses the importance of keeping your word. Numbers 30:1-2 states:

> [1] Moses spoke to the heads of the tribes of the people of Israel, saying, "This is what the Lord has commanded.
> [2] If a man vows a vow to the Lord, or swears an oath to bind himself by a pledge, he shall not break his word. He shall do according to all that proceeds out of his mouth.

Rahab asks for a covenant commitment from the two spies. She wants the spies to swear that they will treat her and her family kindly as she has treated them with kindness. The word "kindness" found twice in verse 12 is the Hebrew word "chesed." It can be translated: "Kindness born out of loyalty to a cause." This is a very important Old Testament concept. One Bible expert said that this word is "one of the richest, most theologically insightful terms in the Old Testament. It is a word that expresses kindness, love, loyalty, and mercy."[3] Chesed is a steadfast love that is based on a covenantal relationship. God is the perfect example of this rock-solid faithfulness that endures forever. In the twenty-six verses of Psalm 136, the word "chesed" is used to describe the Lord in a repeated refrain with the phrase: "His steadfast love endures forever."

When Rahab showed "chesed" to the two spies, she requested that they show "chesed" in return. With the same faithfulness of the promises of God, Rahab wanted these two spies to keep their word. This was a powerful moment between the spies and Rahab as they sought a covenant promise between them. It is fitting that as the nation of Israel prepares to step into the promises of God, a Canaanite prostitute is asking for a covenant promise of loving-kindness.

Rahab asked for a "sure sign" of this steadfast love and kindness. This sign will be a scarlet cord that we will discuss further in tomorrow's devotion. But suffice to say, this sign will be a vivid symbol of faith that is still talked about today.

The two spies agree to the covenant with these profound words: "Our life for yours even to death!" "Our life for yours" meant they promised to value Rahab's life as much as they valued their own. "Even to death" meant they would keep their covenant promise to Rahab even if it killed them.

The God of everlasting love and kindness made the same promise to His children. He sent His only Son to die for our sins. Jesus valued our forgiveness more than His own life. Paul describes Jesus in Philippians 2:8 with these words: "And being found in human form, he humbled himself by becoming obedient to the point of death, even death on a cross."

After some requirements for the covenant are mentioned, the spies close out their promise with this phrase: ". . . we will deal kindly and faithfully with you." The spies return Rahab's "chesed" statement with one of their own. The word here in verse 14 is also "chesed." When you have been shown the "chesed" love of a promise-making, promise-keeping God, you have the integrity and strength to show this faithful love to others.

Questions:

1. How do you feel about God's "chesed" love and faithfulness?

2. In what ways is God's love easier to receive than it is to extend?

3. How are you personally living out your covenant commitment with Jesus Christ?

4. What are your thoughts about "chesed" expressed in the following Scripture?

Exodus 20:4-6 (ESV)
⁴ "You shall not make for yourself a carved image, or any likeness of anything that is in heaven above, or that is in the earth beneath, or that is in the water under the earth. ⁵ You shall not bow down to them or serve them, for I the Lord your God am a jealous God, visiting the iniquity of the fathers on the children to the third and the fourth generation of those who hate me, ⁶ but showing **<u>steadfast love</u>** to thousands of those who love me and keep my commandments.

Day Twelve

Joshua

Faithful and Blameless

Never be afraid to entrust an unknown future
to an all-knowing God.
Anonymous[1]

Text: Joshua 2:15-18

[15] Then she let them down by a rope through the window, for her house was built into the city wall, so that she lived in the wall. [16] And she said to them, "Go into the hills, or the pursuers will encounter you, and hide there three days until the pursuers have returned. Then afterward you may go your way." [17] The men said to her, "We will be guiltless with respect to this oath of yours that you have made us swear.

[18] Behold, when we come into the land, you shall tie this scarlet cord in the window through which you let us down, and you shall gather into your house your father and mother, your brothers, and all your father's household.

Thoughts:

The spies promise to protect Rahab when Jericho was destroyed. However, she must meet several conditions for this promise to be kept. According to Joshua 2:14, Rahab must keep everything a secret. When the attack takes place, she must gather all her family into her house. And she must hang a scarlet cord from her window.

I'm not sure if we fully understand the position that Rahab was in. Remember, she was a Canaanite prostitute who had worshipped idols most of her life. She had heard of the God of the Israelites, and now she has a tremendous choice to make. Will she keep the conditions set by these two spies? Does she trust the word of these strangers, whom she has just met, who are the enemies of the town she calls home? Does she have enough faith to put her life, and her family's life, in the hands of a God she has only heard about?

We all come to a point in our lives where we must choose faith in Christ or to continue our life of sin. Faith always requires action. James said that faith without action is dead. (See James 2:17.) By definition, "faith is the assurance of things hoped for, the conviction of things not seen." (See Hebrews 11:1.) It is called faith because we must believe in something we haven't seen yet. When was the last time your faith in God caused you to make a choice as dangerous as Rahab's? Her choice would mean life or death for her and her family.

Rahab's faith would be proven by her actions. If she believed in the God of Israel, she would hang a scarlet cord from her window. Her salvation would be tied to her faith through a scarlet cord. Even her family would have a choice of faith to make. Would they trust in what Rahab believed and stay in the house knowing their city would soon be destroyed? Her family would show great faith to stay in her house when the walls came tumbling down!

The cord hanging from Rahab's window would be the only way Joshua and the nation of Israel would recognize her house as the one to be spared. It would be a remarkable scene when Israel's army saw a scarlet cord tied to a window when all the dust settled after Jericho collapsed! If you were standing in the rubble and saw this cord, you would have seen it as a symbol of deliverance.

Rahab has a choice to make, and the spies have a commitment to keep. If Rahab doesn't keep her side of the commitment, the spies will not be guilty of her death. In fact, three times in this latter half of Joshua Chapter 2, the spies tell Rahab, "We shall be guiltless." (See verses 17, 19, 20.) The word for "guiltless" found in these three verses is a word that means "free from guilt, clean, and innocent." In other words, it means "blameless." This word is found only eight times in the entire Old Testament, yet three times in this chapter of Joshua. The spies wanted Rahab to understand completely their innocence if she did not choose to put her faith in God. They would be blameless when it came to the death of her and her family if she did not have the scarlet cord hanging from her window.

Likewise, our salvation requires a choice of faith. As the scarlet cord signified Rahab's faith and sealed her rescue, so our trust in the sinless life, sacrificial death, and victorious resurrection of Jesus Christ determines our salvation.

When we choose to believe and act in faith, we can know that God always keeps His promises. If we fail to put our faith in God for salvation, we cannot blame Him for the consequences. Jesus Christ paid the price for our sins at Calvary so that, by faith, we could one day stand before God blameless. 2 Corinthians 5:21 declares, "For our sake He made Him to be sin who knew no sin, so that in Him we might become the righteousness of God." Christ took on our sin so that we stand before God free from guilt, clean, and innocent.

As Rahab hung a scarlet thread from her window and was saved, I trust in Jesus Christ's death for my salvation. As the army of Israel saw the scarlet cord as deliverance, may the world see my life of faith as proof that God has rescued me. Today's Scripture is all about being "Faithful and Blameless." We must live by faith if we are to be found blameless.

Questions:

1. What are your initial thoughts on Rahab hanging a scarlet thread from her window?

2. If you were Rahab, how quickly would you have hung the cord from your window after the spies departed? How many times would you have checked the cord in your window in the days leading up to the destruction of Jericho? Would you have been tempted to take your family and run, rather than trust in such a risky plan? Describe your thoughts.

3. How is your faith in the death and resurrection of Jesus similar to Rahab hanging the scarlet cord out of her window?

Day Thirteen

Joshua

Great Faith Leads to Immediate Obedience

You have not really learned a commandment until you have
obeyed it. The church suffers today from Christians who know
volumes more than they practice.
Vance Havner[1]

Text: Joshua 2:19-21
[19] Then if anyone goes out of the doors of your house into the
street, his blood shall be on his own head, and we shall be guiltless. But if a hand is laid on anyone who is with you in the house,
his blood shall be on our head. [20] But if you tell this business of
ours, then we shall be guiltless with respect to your oath that
you have made us swear." [21] And she said, "According to your
words, so be it." Then she sent them away, and they departed.
And she tied the scarlet cord in the window.

Thoughts:
Rahab agreed to the conditions of the agreement
proposed by the two spies. She responded with these words,
"According to your words, so be it." I love the fact that she told
them to hide for three days for safety, but she went ahead
and tied the scarlet cord in her window for her protection.
She knew that the attack on Jericho couldn't occur until after
the spies reported to their leadership. The army wouldn't
know to spare her and her family unless the spies reported to
them about the scarlet cord. Yet she tied the scarlet cord in
the window. If it was up to me, I too would have tied it in the

window the minute they left. Why wait until later to ensure your salvation?

When God gives us His commands, we are often tempted to delay our response. We rationalize in our minds reasons why God would tell us to do certain things instead of quickly obeying Him. We want to completely understand, up front, everything God is doing when He desires for us to obey Him fully by faith. It is a sign of spiritual maturity when we obey Him quickly.

Any parent can relate to this truth. You get tired of telling your children the same thing repeatedly, and they refuse to obey. You want to protect them, and you know what is best for them. If they would obey, they would quickly find out that you have a loving reason behind your firm commands. When children are young, they resist obeying their parents' commands. When they do obey, often it is after repeated prompts to comply. A sign of maturity is when children obey immediately when they are told to do something. An even larger indicator of development occurs when they do what they are supposed to without being told.

God's Word has a lot to say about obedience. More specifically, God repeatedly spoke to the nation of Israel about the need to obey. Notice His words found in Deuteronomy 28:1-2.

> "¹And if you faithfully obey the voice of the Lord your God, being careful to do all his commandments that I command you today, the Lord your God will set you high above all the nations of the earth. ²And all these blessings shall come upon you and overtake you, if you obey the voice of the Lord your God."

God wants the best for His children, and obeying Him leads to a fulfilled life. The nation of Israel would suffer great consequences because of disobedience and delayed obedience.

What would have happened if Rahab didn't take the spies seriously? What if she didn't hang the scarlet thread out of her window? Or what if she planned on waiting for several weeks to obey while she prayed about it more? If Rahab delayed in her obedience, the consequences would have been deadly.

Rahab's prompt obedience saved her family, but it also would have impacted the entire nation of Israel. Picture the scene: For six days, the army of Israel will march around the city of Jericho. On the seventh day, they will walk around it seven times. Before the walls of Jericho come tumbling down, Israel will have hiked around the city walls thirteen times. Imagine the scene. On day one, a soldier from Israel's army notices a scarlet thread hanging out the window of a house. This cord runs down the entire wall and touches the ground. He points it out to others next to him. Word quickly spreads and, by the second day, everyone notices it as they pass by. Reports come back through the army to protect the family in the home that the cord hangs from. That scarlet cord is a signal for a rescue. Now, every time they march around the city of Jericho, everyone notices that scarlet cord. It gives goosebumps to warriors and chills to the clergy. They know what this cord represents, and they can't walk by without staring. Soon the army of Israel will view the scarlet cord in a more meaningful light. When the walls of Jericho were reduced to rubble, except where this scarlet cord hung, they would be in awe. The soldiers and priests from Israel would look at this cord like the first responders viewed the American flags flying at ground zero after the attacks of 9-11.

Psalm 119:60 says, "I hasten and do not delay to keep your commandments." May we learn a valuable lesson from today's Scripture. When God gives us His commands, let's be quick to obey. Our act of obedience may have ripple effects on others that we couldn't have foreseen. Great faith does lead to immediate obedience that impacts the world for Jesus Christ!

Questions:

1. Why is partial obedience really disobedience?

2. How is delayed obedience actually disobedience?

3. Think over your life and whether there has ever been a time you delayed obedience or only partially obeyed. What consequences did you experience? What impact did it have on others, if any?"

4. In what ways is the size of your faith connected to your level of obedience?

Day Fourteen

Joshua

Don't Lose Sight of the Mission

Every mission needs a missionary!
Anonymous

Text: Joshua 2:22-24
²² They departed and went into the hills and remained there three days until the pursuers returned, and the pursuers searched all along the way and found nothing. ²³ Then the two men returned. They came down from the hills and passed over and came to Joshua the son of Nun, and they told him all that had happened to them. ²⁴ And they said to Joshua, "Truly the Lord has given all the land into our hands. And also, all the inhabitants of the land melt away because of us."

Thoughts:
During the entire journey, the spies never lost sight of their mission. They had entered enemy land with their eyes set on the victory that God had for them. In the pursuit of one mission, they encountered another – they saw the desperate need of Rahab and her family. They did not compromise their convictions. They did not give in to temptation. They remained faithful to God's cause, while at the same time, showing kindness to a prostitute who protected them. These spies did not view Rahab as a prostitute with a bad reputation. Rather, they saw her as someone who desperately needed salvation.

The spies are obedient to Rahab's commands. They hide in the hills for three days (that is, the rest of the first day, and two days thereafter), returning safely to Joshua in Shittim as the three days set in Joshua 1:10 draw to a close. They report to Joshua "everything that had happened" (v. 23). This may well include realities of warfare: numbers, fortifications, and preparations within Jericho. But nothing of this is recorded. Only the words gained from Rahab, the woman who read the news, her own people, and the God of Israel rightly. "The LORD has surely given the whole land into our hands; all the people are melting in fear because of us" (vs. 24). To her words they have added their own "surely." Perhaps this reflects their experience in Jericho. If God could so orchestrate their meeting with the faithful prostitute, then surely he is indeed working for Israel.[2]

The two spies returned to Joshua with a renewed passion for their mission because of the influence of Rahab's faith. Her words had become their words. They could only add "surely" to the words she had pressed on their hearts. They were certain of their mission and everything about their encounter with Rahab validated their convictions.

The story of Joshua 2 is the story of faithful, committed believers on a mission. And just like the two spies, you and I are on a mission. We too have been sent by God to confront and conquer any obstacle to inherit all that He has spiritually promised us. Our enemy is against this mission. Like the spies, we too are sent behind enemy lines. Because we have been sent on a mission, we are all considered missionaries. Perhaps you never thought of yourself as a missionary before, but that's exactly what you are as you live daily for Christ. Your mission field is right where you live and work. God has placed you where you are for His purpose and plan.

Nowhere in Joshua 2 will you read that the two spies compromised their mission. They could have easily rationalized a life of sin while in enemy territory. They could have blended in, stayed awhile, and lost sight of their purpose for going into Canaan. It would have been easy to justify partying a while before going home. No one would know what they did if they kept quiet about it. Yet, they wouldn't settle for less than God's best for their lives. They lived boldly with integrity while in the middle of enemy territory. They never lost sight of God's plan.

We can learn a lot from the spies and their dedication to the mission of God. Although we live in the world, we are "citizens of heaven" (Philippians 3:20-21). One day Christ will return to finish what He started in His death and resurrection: the final redemption of creation, the reversal of the curse, and bringing heaven and earth together forever. While we wait for that glorious day, God has a plan to make a difference in us and through us for His glory now! Living out His plan has present implications and eternal consequences.

Our choice to live on mission for God impacts those around us. Joshua and the people of Israel would have been encouraged by the report from his two spies. When we are obedient to live on mission, others are encouraged to live on mission also. Courage and commitment are contagious.

Questions:

1. Have you ever considered yourself a "missionary" for Christ in enemy territory? Why or why not?

2. In what ways are you compromising your mission?
In what ways are you achieving your mission?

3. What spiritual disciplines do you need to regularly deploy so you won't lose sight of His mission for your life?

4. In what ways are you encouraged by others who are living on mission for Jesus? How are others motivated by your faith?

Day Fifteen

Joshua

Delays and Distance

Seeming delays frequently have the greater purpose
of refining and deepening our faith.
David Jackman[1]

Text: Joshua 3:1-6

[1] Then Joshua rose early in the morning and they set out from Shittim. And they came to the Jordan, he and all the people of Israel, and lodged there before they passed over. [2] At the end of three days the officers went through the camp [3] and commanded the people, "As soon as you see the ark of the covenant of the Lord your God being carried by the Levitical priests, then you shall set out from your place and follow it. [4] Yet there shall be a distance between you and it, about 2,000 cubits in length. Do not come near it, in order that you may know the way you shall go, for you have not passed this way before." [5] Then Joshua said to the people, "Consecrate yourselves, for tomorrow the Lord will do wonders among you." [6] And Joshua said to the priests, "Take up the ark of the covenant and pass on before the people." So they took up the ark of the covenant and went before the people.

Thoughts:

Nobody likes delays. I don't know a single person who loves to wait. I believe our society is more impatient than it has ever been. We want our food ready in less than five minutes, the traffic light to change in five seconds, and our problems to go away instantly. How quickly do you get frustrated when your internet connection isn't as fast as you expected?

Impatience causes us to overcomplicate everything. Our unwillingness to wait also cost us the ability to enjoy the present. It reinforces negative emotions and leaves people frustrated. It also causes many people to rush into mistakes.

Thomas Jefferson once said, "Delay is preferable to error."

Joshua 3 records the people of Israel finally reaching their destination after forty years of wilderness wanderings. They finally came to the Jordan River and set up camp just opposite the Promised Land. Then they must wait for three days! For 72 hours, they hear the rushing waters of the Jordan. For 4,320 minutes, they have experienced the waters of the Jordan outside of its banks.

If the waiting isn't stressful enough, they probably feel tense when they hear the game plan for crossing the flooded river. Their priest must carry the ark of the covenant and step into the fast-moving river. Then the people are to follow them from a great distance. Can you imagine being in that group of people and waiting to finally reach your Promised Land? The anticipation mixed with frustration must have been at an all-time high!

If we approach times of waiting with patience, God can use them for great moments of spiritual preparation. God has a way of growing our faith during moments of great obstacles and long delays. In Joshua 3:5, with one day of waiting remaining, Joshua tells the people to consecrate themselves. Being set apart takes time. Holiness doesn't happen in our lives instantaneously. Spiritual preparation is a gradual development. Following Jesus requires a steady focus.

At the end of their three-day preparation to cross the Jordan, the people of Israel are told to wait in one last very small, but very important, way: they must wait for the ark of the covenant to cross the Jordan ahead of them. The ark of the covenant was a symbol of God's presence throughout the Old Testament. The priests would carry the symbol of God's presence with them as they crossed over the Jordan. The people were to follow the presence of God, but at a distance. Specifically, the people had to stay 2,000 cubits behind God's presence. (See Joshua 3:4.) In biblical times, a cubit was the distance between the elbow and the tip of the middle finger. For the average person, this measured just under two feet. Scholars tell us that 2,000 cubits were roughly 1,000 yards. The people must stay behind the ark of the covenant and follow God from a distance of ten football fields.

Stephen Lennox describes the reason for this great distance in his commentary on Joshua:

> No closer than half a mile from God's presence. As with so many other passages in Scripture, this tiny detail reveals much. By requiring this distance between the ark and the Israelites, God reinforced the truth that while He is wholly Other, even dangerously so, He willingly comes near for the good of His people. The Israelites were able to be close—within one thousand yards—but not too close for their own good. God reveals Himself even while he conceals Himself.
>
> This is the paradox of knowing God, both then and now. Although too holy to approach, we can experience His blessed presence if we faithfully obey. We can know him, but only "through a glass, darkly" (1 Corinthians 13:12). As Thomas Aquinas put it, "the more perfectly we know God in this life, the more we understand that He surpasses all that the mind comprehends."[2]

The distance from God's presence would give His people both reverence and perspective. It would also allow them to see a miracle before they experienced one. Delays and distance can be great opportunities for developing patience, growing spiritually, and witnessing the wonderful works of our marvelous God.

Questions:

1. Why is it so difficult for you to wait?

2. How can Psalm 46:10 encourage you in your times of waiting?

> "Be still, and know that I am God. I will be exalted among the nations, I will be exalted in the earth!"

3. How do you follow God closely while also respecting Him greatly?

Day Sixteen

Joshua

Faith to Step Out

Faith is not believing in spite of the evidence;
it is obeying in spite of the consequences.
Skip Heitzig[1]

Text: Joshua 3:7-13

⁷ The Lord said to Joshua, "Today I will begin to exalt you in the sight of all Israel, that they may know that, as I was with Moses, so I will be with you. ⁸ And as for you, command the priests who bear the ark of the covenant, 'When you come to the brink of the waters of the Jordan, you shall stand still in the Jordan.'" ⁹ And Joshua said to the people of Israel, "Come here and listen to the words of the Lord your God." ¹⁰ And Joshua said, "Here is how you shall know that the living God is among you and that he will without fail drive out from before you the Canaanites, the Hittites, the Hivites, the Perizzites, the Girgashites, the Amorites, and the Jebusites.

¹¹ Behold, the ark of the covenant of the Lord of all the earth is passing over before you into the Jordan. ¹² Now therefore take twelve men from the tribes of Israel, from each tribe a man.

¹³ And when the soles of the feet of the priests bearing the ark of the Lord, the Lord of all the earth, shall rest in the waters of the Jordan, the waters of the Jordan shall be cut off from flowing, and the waters coming down from above shall stand in one heap."

Thoughts:

In some ways, this miracle of crossing the Jordan compares with the crossing of the Red Sea found in Exodus 14. Both miracles involved crossing water that had been divided by the hand of God. Both miracles also involved the people crossing over on dry ground. Crossing the Red Sea and the Jordan River both consisted of people moving toward all that God had promised them. And obviously, both miracles required great faith from the people as they crossed over.

However, there are many differences between the two crossings. In the Red Sea encounter, the water was parted as Moses stretched out his hand over the sea. It took all night long for the sea to be parted and the passage on dry ground to be ready. (See Exodus 14:21.) However, here in Joshua 3, the water only divided when the priests carrying the ark of the covenant stepped into the flooded river. When the priests stepped out in faith, the water stopped flowing instantly, and the priests immediately stood on dry ground. In addition, at the crossing of the Jordan, the priests stood in the middle of the river on dry ground as all the people passed by.

The one big difference between the two crossings is that the ark of the covenant was central to the crossing of the Jordan River. As we discussed in yesterday's devotion, the ark of the covenant was a symbol of God's presence with the people. From this, we learn that we cannot cross over to the life God has for us unless we continue to walk with Jesus every day. Alan Redpath shares the following insight:

> That ark went on in front, and whereas until then the whole army had been perplexed and in despair as they gazed at the impossible river, now their thoughts were centered on the fact that the Lord was with them, as symbolized by the ark of the covenant. As they saw the ark go

into the river, the waters parted, the riverbed became dry, and the impossibility was overcome!

What has this to teach us? That Jesus the Savior one day went into the Garden of Gethsemane, where the flood rolled before Him. Then He went to a cross on a hill of Calvary, where it seemed as if the waters had submerged Him. He died, and they laid Him in a tomb, outside of which was a sealed stone for a door. But that was not all: "Up from the grave He arose, with a mighty triumph o'er His foes." The Lord Jesus, writes Paul, "spoiled principalities and powers and made a spectacle of them openly, triumphing over them" in His resurrection (Colossians 2:15).[2]

At the cross and an empty tomb, Jesus Christ won the victory over sin, death, hell, and the grave. He not only paid the debt for our sins, but He provided a way for us to live in fellowship with the Father. As we follow Christ by faith, we can cross over what was impossible to an abundant life found in a personal relationship with Him.

May the following words from Alan Redpath encourage us to live daily in the presence of Jesus:

Does shame, human nature, temperament, or pride stand between the land of blessing and the Christian like this flooded Jordan? Let a child of God get his eyes on the Lord Jesus and look: between the impossibility and himself there HE is. After that, the child of God does not talk about "getting the victory." It isn't the victory he wants; it is the Victor. He does not speak about "striving for a new blessing" and "seeking to enter a new experience." His eyes are on the Lord Jesus, and he puts the Lord Jesus between Himself and the onslaught of the devil, and looks up into His face, and there is victory.

Questions:

1. What level of faith would be required to have been a priest carrying the ark of the covenant in Joshua 3? Imagine what they went through emotionally, physically, and spiritually.

2. What level of faith would be required to be one of the leaders from each of the twelve tribes of Israel?

3. What level of faith would be needed to be a part of the crowd that day? What impact do you think their view of the priest standing on dry ground with the ark of the covenant had on their faith to cross over?

4. How can you increasingly grow in your faith by trusting in His presence?

Day Seventeen

Joshua

Overcoming Great Obstacles

Progress also involves risk.
You can't steal second and keep your foot on first.
Frederick Wilcox[1]

Text: Joshua 3:14-17

¹⁴ So when the people set out from their tents to pass over the Jordan with the priests bearing the ark of the covenant before the people, ¹⁵ and as soon as those bearing the ark had come as far as the Jordan, and the feet of the priests bearing the ark were dipped in the brink of the water (now the Jordan overflows all its banks throughout the time of harvest), ¹⁶ the waters coming down from above stood and rose up in a heap very far away, at Adam, the city that is beside Zarethan, and those flowing down toward the Sea of the Arabah, the Salt Sea, were completely cut off. And the people passed over opposite Jericho. ¹⁷ Now the priests bearing the ark of the covenant of the Lord stood firmly on dry ground in the midst of the Jordan, and all Israel was passing over on dry ground until all the nation finished passing over the Jordan.

Thoughts:

What obstacle stands between you and your Promised Land? What barrier do you need to cross in order to live in the promises of God? Do you have enough faith in God to trust Him to help you get there?

Those are questions that Israel had to come to grips with in Joshua 3. Interestingly, the Lord brought the people of Israel to this normally quiet river at harvest time. At harvest time, the Jordan River was overflowing its banks. All the waters had come down from the mountains, flooding that area. Remember, the people of Israel were camped at that very spot for three days. If we are to see a spiritual harvest in our lives, we are going to have to cross some hurdles too!

The Hebrew word in verse 1 for "crossed over" or "passed over," depending on your translation, is the word "abar." It means more than just getting from point A to point B. "Abar" means a very significant moment of time. It means "passing out of what you've been accustomed to into something brand new for which you have no plans or precedent." Essentially, God was telling the Israelites, "Your past is now finished. The wilderness journeys are over. There is something brand new that I have for you. It is on the other side of the river. It is time to cross over!"

We must not miss the magnitude of this event for the nation of Israel. A tremendous amount of testing had brought them to this moment. They failed the tests many times, and the consequences had delayed their trip. Now that they were finally at the river crossing, they had a lot to look back on and much to look forward to.

Notice how the following Scripture details their journey:

Deuteronomy 8:2-5 (ESV)
² And you shall remember the whole way that the Lord your God has led you these forty years in the wilderness, that he might humble you, testing you to know what was in your heart, whether you would keep his commandments or not. ³ And he humbled you and let you hunger and fed you with manna, which you did not know, nor did your fathers know, that he might make you know that man does not live by bread alone, but man lives by every word that comes from the mouth of the Lord. ⁴ Your clothing did not wear out on you and your foot

did not swell these forty years. ⁵ Know then in your heart that, as a man disciplines his son, the Lord your God disciplines you.

God has tested the nation of Israel and provided for them the entire wilderness journey, teaching them to depend on Him. For forty years in the difficulties of treacherous lands, their clothes never wore out. In all their travels by foot, their million-plus pairs of feet were never swollen. God had truly been faithful to them, even when they hadn't always been faithful to Him. His presence is always there, and He is always able to fulfill His promises.

In yesterday's devotion, we highlighted the importance of the ark of the covenant. The ark of the covenant is mentioned seven times in this chapter of Joshua. The ark was that special piece of Tabernacle furniture that symbolized the presence and power of God. When the ark was in the Holy of Holies, the glory of God rested upon the special lid called the mercy seat. To Israel, it represented God's presence in the midst of His people. His presence to all believers is a sign of His mercy.

The presence of God was symbolized through the ark just as it was pictured in the cloud by day and pillar of fire by night. God's presence was found wherever the ark traveled. When God moved, the ark and the people were to move. When God stopped, they were to do the same.

There is a valuable spiritual lesson here. When we face barriers to our Promised Land, be sensitive to the movement of the Lord. When He says move, follow Him! The same God that parts the Red Sea and the Jordan River can part your problems and take you through!

Questions:

1. What obstacles are you completely depending on God to overcome?

2. In what tangible ways can you focus more on His presence to give you greater confidence in His victory?

3. In what specific ways has He guided you and provided for you in your past journeys with Him?

Day Eighteen

Joshua

Don't Forget to Remember

The stones were to tell the other nations round about that this
God is different. He really exists; He is a living God, a God of real
power who is immanent in the world.
Francis Schaeffer [1]

Text: Joshua 4:1-10

[1] When all the nation had finished passing over the Jordan,
the Lord said to Joshua, [2] "Take twelve men from the people,
from each tribe a man, [3] and command them, saying, 'Take
twelve stones from here out of the midst of the Jordan, from the
very place where the priests' feet stood firmly, and bring them
over with you and lay them down in the place where you lodge
tonight.'" [4] Then Joshua called the twelve men from the people
of Israel, whom he had appointed, a man from each tribe. [5] And
Joshua said to them, "Pass on before the ark of the Lord your
God into the midst of the Jordan, and take up each of you a stone
upon his shoulder, according to the number of the tribes of the
people of Israel, [6] that this may be a sign among you. When your
children ask in time to come, 'What do those stones mean to
you?' [7] then you shall tell them that the waters of the Jordan
were cut off before the ark of the covenant of the Lord. When it
passed over the Jordan, the waters of the Jordan were cut off.
So these stones shall be to the people of Israel a memorial forever." [8] And the people of Israel did just as Joshua commanded
and took up twelve stones out of the midst of the Jordan, according to the number of the tribes of the people of Israel, just

as the Lord told Joshua. And they carried them over with them to the place where they lodged and laid them down there. ⁹ And Joshua set up twelve stones in the midst of the Jordan, in the place where the feet of the priests bearing the ark of the covenant had stood; and they are there to this day. ¹⁰ For the priests bearing the ark stood in the midst of the Jordan until everything was finished that the Lord commanded Joshua to tell the people, according to all that Moses had commanded Joshua. The people passed over in haste.

Thoughts:

This fourth chapter of Joshua is about remembering! While there are some things we need to remember to forget, there are moments we forget to remember! Sometimes we need to look back at His provision so that we can be reminded to look forward to His presence, in order to live in the present with His power!

God tells the Israelites to take 12 stones from the dry riverbed and place them as a monument and testimony of God's sovereignty.

Note that these stones were taken out of the deepest part in the middle of the riverbed. I truly believe that our strongest memorials will come from the deepest parts of our lives. Our hardest moments could actually become our highest memorials. The stones in the middle of our deepest pain can become the greatest statements of God's goodness.

And notice that these stones were "to be a memorial to the people of Israel forever." I need memories that will outlive me. My children don't necessarily need another sermon as much as they need some stones! They need some reminders of when God showed up in power. They need a testimony of His strength during the tests of my weakness. They need something they can see that will say something about who He is and all that He has done!!

I don't know about you, but I don't do a very good job creating monuments to the memories of the goodness of God for my family to remember. I mean, I have the 12 stones. Really, I do! In our backyard, in front of the cross a special family friend built for us, we have 12 stacked stones. They even have a light on them! But I haven't used them to shed light on all that God has done.

"God help me to create some memorials so that others might be encouraged, my children might be educated, and the whole world might be enlightened to who You are!" We have a God who has done great things! And those things are worth remembering!

Don't miss what happens in Joshua 4:9. While the twelve men would set up a visible memorial in Gilgal, Joshua set up a hidden memorial in the midst of the Jordan River. Joshua would take twelve stones and place them right where the priests stood holding the ark of the covenant. The waters of the Jordan would eventually cover these stones. So the question arises: Why set up a memorial that no one can see? I believe the answer is that sometimes you need special moments with God where you have clearly realized His presence. Those twelve stones that Joshua laid down were Joshua's way of worshipping God. The twelve stones in Gilgal would be a memorial for all to remember God's power. The twelve stones amid the Jordan River would be Joshua's way to highlight his personal experience of God's presence and power. The stones laid by the twelve men would be for remembrance. The stones placed by Joshua would be for reverence.

May we each set "stones" in place to help us remember to remind others of all that He has done. May they also cause you to stop and worship His presence in your life.

Questions:

1. What is God doing in your life that is worth remembering?

2. What legacy are you leaving your children concerning all that God has done?

3. What do your neighbors know about your God by the moments you have memorialized?

4. When was the last time you experienced Jesus' presence in such a powerful way that it caused you to stop and demonstrate your love for Him? If not, why not seek Him now?

Day Nineteen

Joshua

___

Battle Ready in the Midst of Miracles

Salvation is a helmet, not a nightcap.
Vance Havner[1]

Our tent is pitched not in paradise,
But on a field of battle.
LE Maxwell[2]

Text: Joshua 4:11-14

[11] And when all the people had finished passing over, the ark of the Lord and the priests passed over before the people. [12] The sons of Reuben and the sons of Gad and the half-tribe of Manasseh passed over armed before the people of Israel, as Moses had told them. [13] About 40,000 ready for war passed over before the Lord for battle, to the plains of Jericho. [14] On that day the Lord exalted Joshua in the sight of all Israel, and they stood in awe of him just as they had stood in awe of Moses, all the days of his life.

Thoughts:

The nation of Israel crossed over the Jordan River into the Promised Land. They had crossed over because of God's miraculous power and His faithfulness to keep His promise. Joshua 4:12 details that two and a half tribes of Israel crossed over: "armed before the people of Israel . . . ready for war," and "for battle." It is interesting to note that these 40,000 men were armed as they crossed the Jordan. All the people knew they would face more battles in the Promised Land. There would be seven nations to overcome and constant battles to face.

Spiritual victories precede future battles. When God takes you through your obstacles and leads you towards His will, the devil will attack. Even as the miracle is taking place, always stay armed for battle. Never rest on the miracles of God until you are in Heaven and your enemy is forever defeated.

Joshua 4:13 states that the "Lord exalted Joshua" on the day Israel crossed over. God assured the people that they could trust their leader Joshua just as they trusted Moses. The nation of Israel would need godly leadership. They would need a courageous general to lead them into battle and keep them focused on God's plan. Every time they called their leader by name, they were reminded that "God Saves."

When God exalts a leader, it is for the benefit of His people. God never raises up a leader so that the leader can be praised. God elevates a leader to accomplish His purposes and bring glory to His name. We need more godly and courageous leaders focused on God and ready for battle.

God has a unique way of fulfilling His will. His place and timing are always perfect. He works on a divine schedule, chooses people for a specific purpose, and picks certain places for special reasons.

This special event would mark a special place for a future journey with Jesus. Between approximately 26-29 AD, a man came down from Jerusalem and began baptizing in the Jordan River. John's Gospel tells us the area where John the Baptist was baptizing.

John 1:25-28 (ESV)
[25] They asked him, "Then why are you baptizing, if you are neither the Christ, nor Elijah, nor the Prophet?" [26] John answered them, "I baptize with water, but among you stands one you do

not know, ²⁷ even he who comes after me, the strap of whose sandal I am not worthy to untie." ²⁸ These things took place in Bethany across the Jordan, where John was baptizing.

In verse 28, the oldest manuscripts have the word "bethabara" for the word translated "Bethany." The Greek word "Bethabara" comes from "Beth," which means "place" or "house," and "abar," which means "crossing." So "bethabara" can be translated, "the house of passage or the place of crossing." Many people believe that John the Baptist was baptizing people in the Jordan River at the place where the nation of Israel crossed the Jordan 1500 years before.

Only our God could orchestrate the details of the crossing to bring future glory to His name. John the Baptist, the forerunner of Jesus, would baptize people at the same place that a man whose name means, "God is Salvation," would lead God's people to the place God promised. This reminds me of Abraham's willingness to offer Isaac at the same mountain that Father God would offer His only Son for our salvation. Make no mistake, Jesus saves, and God cares about the details of your life. He leads you to where He chooses because His plan is flawless. God also leads you to who He desires so that you can make a difference in their lives for His glory.

Questions:

1. How do you stay battle-ready as you experience spiritual victory? What part do you think your spiritual readiness for warfare plays in the future victories God has in store for your life?

2. In what ways can you grow as a leader to be all that God has called you to be? Who has God specifically called you to lead?

3. How does the place of John the Baptist's baptism give you more faith that God is in control of the details of life?

Day Twenty

Joshua

Out, Through, and Onward

What could be on the other side of your "Yes" to God?
Lysa TerKeurst[1]

Text: Joshua 4:15-18

15 And the Lord said to Joshua, 16 "Command the priests bearing the ark of the testimony to come up out of the Jordan." 17 So Joshua commanded the priests, "Come up out of the Jordan." 18 And when the priests bearing the ark of the covenant of the Lord came up from the midst of the Jordan, and the soles of the priests' feet were lifted up on dry ground, the waters of the Jordan returned to their place and overflowed all its banks, as before.

Thoughts:

Imagine being one of the priests and hearing Joshua's command, "Come up out of the Jordan." From your vantage point, you have watched crowds of people walk by as you have nervously held the ark of the covenant. You would have been filled with an unbelievable range of emotions. Holding the symbol of God's presence would have filled you with both great fear and awe. Watching the faces of the nation as they passed by must have flooded your soul with joy amid the miraculous power of God. The faces of the people would have been contagious, and the smiles would have been endless. You would want to high-five them, but you'd be clinging to the ark.

The first question that comes to mind is, "How long did they stand holding the ark of the covenant waiting for the people to cross over?" The answer to that question depends on how many people crossed over. Joshua 4:14 states that 40,000 armed soldiers passed over. But that number seems to be just the fighting men of the two-and-a-half tribes that settled east of the Promised Land.

Numbers 26 recorded the census of the men who were of fighting age before to the crossing:

Numbers 26:1-4, 51 (ESV)
[1] After the plague, the Lord said to Moses and to Eleazar the son of Aaron, the priest, [2] "Take a census of all the congregation of the people of Israel, from twenty years old and upward, by their fathers' houses, all in Israel who are able to go to war." [3] And Moses and Eleazar the priest spoke with them in the plains of Moab by the Jordan at Jericho, saying, [4] "Take a census of the people, from twenty years old and upward," as the Lord commanded Moses . . . [51] This was the list of the people of Israel, 601,730.

600,000 people, and that is just the fighting men. Scholars estimate that if you included women, children, priests, and the elderly, at least 2.5 million Israelites crossed the Jordan River on dry ground! And that doesn't include all the livestock that had to cross with them.

If it took each person just one second to cross over, it would have taken 2.5 million people 29 days to cross. However, Joshua 3:16 gives clear details as to where the water was cut off in both directions. God gives Israel a twenty-mile stretch of dry riverbed to cross over. We can't know how many crossed at a time or how long it took for the entire nation to cross over on dry ground. This discussion is just to stress how enormous this event was for all involved. But now those words mean just a little more – "Come up out of the Jordan."

The priests were about to have another unbelievable encounter. Joshua 4:18 said that as soon as the soles of their feet touched the dry ground of the bank outside the Jordan, the waters returned to their place. As soon as they stepped out, the river was flooded again. Imagine what they felt as they watched the place where they had just stood engulfed with waves of water again.

The entire nation of Israel witnessed the miracle of God's power as they crossed the Jordan. Yet nobody had a closer seat to the action than the priests. The waters didn't stop until they first got their feet wet. Notice the progression of events for the priests: They went from balancing the ark on their shoulders, to stepping into the flooded river, to standing on dry ground, to holding the ark while all the people crossed over, to stepping out on dry ground, and finally seeing the riverbed flooded with water again.

It has been said that leaders must battle where the fighting is fiercest because they are on the front row of the fight. Leading with Jesus puts a target on your back from the enemy. However, stepping up to lead in God's kingdom work also has incredible rewards. Leaders get to see God's miracles from the greatest vantage points.

Crossing the Jordan entails great spiritual truths for our lives today. For God to bring us out, through, and onward, we must be willing to step out in faith. God brought the Israelites out of bondage, through their obstacles, and onward to their Promised Land. Likewise, we can witness God's deliverance from our own wilderness wanderings. If we walk by faith, God can take us through any obstacles we may face. If we surrender to Him daily and trust Him fully, Jesus can take us onward to greater places in our spiritual lives.

Questions:

1. What obstacles are you currently struggling with that you must trust Jesus to bring you through?

2. How much faith do you have in Jesus? Do you really believe He can help you move forward in your walk with Him? Mark 9:24 records the words of a hurting father to Jesus: "I believe; help my unbelief." How can you make that your prayer today?

3. Is your walk with Jesus close enough to have a front-row seat for His miracles? If not, what needs to take place for you to draw nearer to God?

Day Twenty-One

Joshua

Living out Your Biblical Responsibility

We will not hide them from their children,
but tell to the coming generation
the glorious deeds of the Lord, and His might,
and the wonders that He has done.
Psalm 78:4

Text: Joshua 4:19-24

¹⁹ The people came up out of the Jordan on the tenth day of the first month, and they encamped at Gilgal on the east border of Jericho. ²⁰ And those twelve stones, which they took out of the Jordan, Joshua set up at Gilgal. ²¹ And he said to the people of Israel, "When your children ask their fathers in times to come, 'What do these stones mean?' ²² then you shall let your children know, 'Israel passed over this Jordan on dry ground.' ²³ For the Lord your God dried up the waters of the Jordan for you until you passed over, as the Lord your God did to the Red Sea, which he dried up for us until we passed over, ²⁴ so that all the peoples of the earth may know that the hand of the Lord is mighty, that you may fear the Lord your God forever."

Thoughts:

Every follower of Jesus Christ has a biblical duty to tell the next generation of the miraculous works of God. Neither God nor the Bible has changed. They both remain the same. Each generation must teach biblical truths to the following generation, or the consequences will be tragic. If the next generation is biblically illiterate, it will be because we did not teach them God's Word. If the generation that follows us doubts God, it will be because we were silent about His power.

In Psalm 145:4, David declared, "One generation shall commend your works to another, and shall declare your mighty acts." If we don't praise His works ourselves and share His mighty acts with others, how will those who follow us ever follow Jesus?

When the nation of Israel got to Gilgal, they set up the twelve stones from the Jordan River as a memorial to God's mighty act of salvation. According to Joshua 4:19-24, those memorial stones served two major purposes. First, the stones were placed in Gilgal to be a conversation starter between parents and children. When the children of future generations saw the stones, they would ask what they meant. When they asked the question, parents would have an open door to tell them about God's awesome power and their miraculous deliverance. The second purpose of the stones was to display God's power to every person on earth. These stones would tell a story down through the ages that would cause people everywhere to fear God.

The generation that had just passed over the Jordan River knew the royal law. It is referred to as the Shema. Their parents and grandparents were given this law by God. This law was placed in small boxes and tied to their foreheads and hands. It went with God's people wherever they went. This law was passed down to them by Moses and recorded in the book of the bible that precedes Joshua.

Deuteronomy 6:4-15 (ESV)

⁴"Hear, O Israel: The Lord our God, the Lord is one. ⁵You shall love the Lord your God with all your heart and with all your soul and with all your might."

⁶ "And these words that I command you today shall be on your heart. ⁷ You shall teach them diligently to your children, and shall talk of them when you sit in your house, and when you walk by the way, and when you lie down, and when you rise. ⁸ You shall bind them as a sign on your hand, and they shall be as frontlets between your eyes. ⁹ You shall write them on the doorposts of your house and on your gates."

¹⁰ "And when the Lord your God brings you into the land that he swore to your fathers, to Abraham, to Isaac, and to Jacob, to give you – with great and good cities that you did not build, ¹¹ and houses full of all good things that you did not fill, and cisterns that you did not dig, and vineyards and olive trees that you did not plant – and when you eat and are full, ¹² then take care lest you forget the Lord, who brought you out of the land of Egypt, out of the house of slavery. ¹³ It is the Lord your God you shall fear. Him you shall serve and by his name you shall swear. ¹⁴ You shall not go after other gods, the gods of the peoples who are around you – ¹⁵ for the Lord your God in your midst is a jealous God – lest the anger of the Lord your God be kindled against you, and he destroy you from off the face of the earth."

We are always one generation away from living in a world that has no faith in God. The greatest detriment to the cause of Christ is parents who say they believe in Christ but do not pass down the message of Christ to their children. Living out our biblical responsibility means commending God's works to the next generation and diligently teaching God's commands to our children.

Questions:

1. What are some things we can do to commend God's work to the next generation?

2. In what ways are you personally teaching God's Word to the generation that follows yours? Are you living up to and living out your spiritual responsibility?

3. Make a list of the major miracles God has done in your life. You could call them your spiritual memorial stones. Share them over the next several weeks with those whom God placed under your leadership. Reread Joshua 4:19-24, Psalm 145:4, and Deuteronomy 6:4-14 regularly to keep your focus on your biblical responsibility.

Day Twenty-Two

Joshua

Fear that Doesn't Lead to Faith

Whosoever will reign with Christ in heaven,
must have Christ reigning with him on earth.
John Wesley[1]

Text: Joshua 5:1

¹ As soon as all the kings of the Amorites who were beyond the Jordan to the west, and all the kings of the Canaanites who were by the sea, heard that the Lord had dried up the waters of the Jordan for the people of Israel until they had crossed over, their hearts melted and there was no longer any spirit in them because of the people of Israel.

Thoughts:

Have you ever been so afraid that you trembled uncontrollably? In our culture, people have all types of phobias. The word "phobia" actually comes from a New Testament word, "phobos." This word means "great fear" or "horror." There is a long list of fears that people have. All these fears end in the word "phobia." For example, hydrophobia literally means a fear of water. Claustrophobia is a fear of confined spaces.

Phobias can cause incredible stress and anxiety. Improper fear can lead to all sorts of physical, emotional, and spiritual problems. I have missed out on a lot of fun experiences with my family because of my claustrophobia. Certain fears are unhealthy, and God can give you victory over them.

95

However, some well-meaning people believe that all fear is wrong. 2 Timothy 1:7 is one of those verses people take out of context to argue against all fear. This Scripture says, "for God gave us a spirit not of fear, but of power and love and self-control." The word for fear in this text means, "coward" or "timid." This verse is not teaching against fear. In 2 Timothy, Paul exhorts Timothy to fan into the flame the gift that God gave him. Paul is challenging Timothy to live out his Christian life with courage and strength. God doesn't give us a weak, cowardly spirit. If we are cowards, that spirit of cowardice did not come from Christ.

However, certain fears can be extremely beneficial. The kings of the Amorites and Canaanites had a healthy fear when they heard that Israel had crossed the Jordan River on dry ground. In Joshua 5:1, Scripture specifically says, ". . . their hearts melted and there was no longer any spirit in them." This phrase literally means, "their hearts dissolved and there was no longer any breath in them." When they heard that God dried up the Jordan, their hopes withered. Every bit of motivation to stand against Israel was gone. Fear took their breath away. They had lost all expectations and anticipations of victory. The kings of the enemies of Israel were completely terrorized and paralyzed with fear.

Have you ever been so afraid of what God can do that your heart melted with fear? Have you ever come to a place in your life where you have stood in awe at the omnipotence of God?

So, not all fear is bad. A proper fear can be a great tool to protect you. For example, if you have a healthy fear of lions, you keep your distance when you see one. Without that respectful fear, you would not take them seriously. This lack of fear could quickly turn deadly.

Scripture teaches that we should fear God. Proverbs 9:10 states, "The fear of the LORD is the beginning of wisdom, and the knowledge of the Holy One is insight." If the fear of God comes before wisdom, then an absence of fear is foolish. You could reason from Proverbs 9:10, "If you do not fear the LORD, you have not started on the path towards wisdom in your life." The second half of that proverb teaches that knowing who God is gives insight. Our understanding of God comes from our reverent fear of who He is. A reverence of God gives us insight into His character. To be wise you must first have a reverent fear of God. Therefore, wisdom begins with the fear of the Lord and leads to the knowledge of His holiness.

The problem with the Amorite and Canaanite kings was their fear of God never led to a faith in God. The miracles of God took their breath away, but they never trusted in Him to take their sins away. There are many people today who are exactly like these kings. They have a fear of what God can do, yet they refuse to put their trust in who God is.

Reverent fear is the beginning point in our journey towards Jesus, but it doesn't automatically lead to a personal relationship with God. Somewhere along their journey regarding wisdom, these kings leaned on their own understanding over their insight into God's holiness. They loved their own power and positions so much that they never took the time to realize the holiness of God. They preferred to be the kings of their own domains rather than surrender to the lordship of the King of kings.

If we are not careful, we will let God take our breath away with His power and still not seek after Him personally. May our hearts still melt in His presence because of His power. And may a reverent fear of who He is lead us to comprehend His holiness. May our great fear lead to a growing faith!

Questions:

1. Have you started the journey towards wisdom with a reverent fear of God?

2. If you do fear God, how has this led to an understanding of His holiness?

3. In what ways has your fear of God led to a greater faith in God?

4. What does John Wesley's quote for today's devotion say to you personally?

Day Twenty-Three

Joshua

The Sign of the Covenant

When we realize that we are children of the covenant,
we know who we are and what God expects of us.
Russell M. Nelson[1]

Text: Joshua 5:2-5

² At that time the Lord said to Joshua, "Make flint knives and circumcise the sons of Israel a second time." ³ So Joshua made flint knives and circumcised the sons of Israel at Gibeath-haaraloth. ⁴ And this is the reason why Joshua circumcised them: all the males of the people who came out of Egypt, all the men of war, had died in the wilderness on the way after they had come out of Egypt. ⁵ Though all the people who came out had been circumcised, yet all the people who were born on the way in the wilderness after they had come out of Egypt had not been circumcised.

Thoughts:

Circumcision was the sign of the covenant that God had given to Abraham 500 years before what is recorded in Joshua 5. God laid out the terms of this covenant in Genesis 17:7-14, and He tied Israel's inheritance of Canaan with their ongoing observance of circumcision:

⁷ "And I will establish my covenant between me and you and your offspring after you throughout their generations for an everlasting covenant, to be God to you and

99

to your offspring after you. [8] And I will give to you and to your offspring after you the land of your sojournings, all the land of Canaan, for an everlasting possession, and I will be their God."

[9] And God said to Abraham, "As for you, you shall keep my covenant, you and your offspring after you throughout their generations. [10] This is my covenant, which you shall keep, between me and you and your offspring after you: Every male among you shall be circumcised. [11] You shall be circumcised in the flesh of your foreskins, and it shall be a sign of the covenant between me and you. [12] He who is eight days old among you shall be circumcised. Every male throughout your generations, whether born in your house or bought with your money from any foreigner who is not of your offspring, [13] both he who is born in your house and he who is bought with your money, shall surely be circumcised. So shall my covenant be in your flesh an everlasting covenant. [14] Any uncircumcised male who is not circumcised in the flesh of his foreskin shall be cut off from his people; he has broken my covenant."

The following Scriptures reveal that Abraham was declared righteous before circumcision:

Genesis 15:6 (ESV)
[6] And he [Abraham] believed the Lord, and he counted it to him as righteousness.

Romans 4:11-12 (ESV)
[11] He received the sign of circumcision as a seal of the righteousness that he had by faith while he was still uncircumcised. The purpose was to make him the father of all who believe without being circumcised, so that righteousness

would be counted to them as well, [12] and to make him the father of the circumcised who are not merely circumcised but who also walk in the footsteps of the faith that our father Abraham had before he was circumcised.

The fact that Abraham was counted righteous by his faith did not discount the sign of the covenant. Circumcision was not optional for the Israelites, but these Scriptures prove that circumcision alone was not enough to make one righteous. In fact, the Exodus generation kept the sign of the covenant outwardly but failed to love God inwardly enough to obey His commands.

Here in our study of Joshua, none of the new generation had been circumcised during the forty years of wilderness wanderings. The older generation, who had been circumcised before the Exodus, had died along the way. Except for Joshua and Caleb, every male over eight days old hadn't been circumcised. While commentators have given all sorts of reasons for not circumcising in the wilderness, the bottom line is Israel had failed to keep their side of the covenant. God in His grace still delivered them to the Promised Land. But now, they must keep the sign of the covenant.

Please don't miss the significance of the sign of the covenant. Signs don't always convey substance. You can keep the sign without obeying your Savior. For instance, you can be baptized and still live in disobedience to God. So, you can observe a ceremony and never have a relationship with Christ. However, if you love Christ with all of your heart, you will have a great desire to obey His commands.

This truth is proven by contrasting the older generation of circumcised men who failed to enter the Promised Land with those who entered the Promised Land and then obeyed the sign of the covenant.

Numbers 14:22-23 describes God's judgment on those who had been circumcised but died in the wilderness:

> [22] none of the men who have seen my glory and my signs that I did in Egypt and in the wilderness, and yet have put me to the test these ten times and have not obeyed my voice, [23] shall see the land that I swore to give to their fathers. And none of those who despised me shall see it.

Joshua 5:6 states these men "perished because they did not obey the voice of the LORD." They had the sign of circumcision, but they missed the blessing of Canaan. The warning in today's devotion is that it is possible to bear all the marks of the people of God but miss the mark when it comes to your personal relationship with Him. May we take God's covenant seriously so that we don't miss out on all that God has for His people.

Questions:

1. What are some covenantal signs God gives to us as Christians?

2. What is your sign of the covenant?

3. Since obedience to God is a matter of the heart and not just outward actions, take some time to reflect on whether you are obeying the Lord wholeheartedly in the present. Are you relying on past observance to His commands instead of obedience now?

4. In what ways do you continue to obey God in your relationship with Him?

Day Twenty-Four

Joshua

Wandering in Disobedience

What one generation tolerates,
the next generation will embrace.
John Wesley[1]

Text: Joshua 5:6

[6] For the people of Israel walked forty years in the wilderness, until all the nation, the men of war who came out of Egypt, perished, because they did not obey the voice of the Lord; the Lord swore to them that he would not let them see the land that the Lord had sworn to their fathers to give to us, a land flowing with milk and honey.

Thoughts:

These men of war perished. At times, they had courage to fight physical battles, but they couldn't conquer their own selfish natures. They saw the Red Sea open by the power of God, but they couldn't continually open their hearts to God. They saw God's presence hovering over Mount Sinai, but they would not surrender to His presence over their lives.

A whole nation wandered for forty years because of disobedience. Their children and grandchildren were denied Promised Land living as punishment for not obeying the voice of the Lord.

If you study the nation of Israel after they entered Canaan, you will discover that this new generation makes some of the same mistakes as their forefathers. This new generation will see victories from God when they obey His voice. And they will experience setbacks and suffering when they disobey His Word. John Wesley was extremely accurate when he said, "What one generation tolerates, the next generation will embrace."

Disobedience hurts on many levels. First, disobedience disrespects God. Every parent knows this feeling. You do everything you can to love your children. You sacrifice and put their needs above your own. You give until it hurts. And then you tell your children to do something for their own good, and they disobey you. Your children suffer consequences that would not have been theirs if they had only obeyed. You had great plans for them, but disobedience has caused them setbacks in their personal lives. If they would have listened and obeyed, they could have been blessed.

Just as disobedience to our earthly parents is disrespectful, disobedience to our Heavenly Father is even more so, for He is our Creator. God sacrificed His only Son to show His love for us and to give us the gift of salvation. What more could our Father have done to show us His incredible love? God has plans for our lives. He has plans to prosper us and not to harm us, to give us a hope and a future, yet we disobey Him and sometimes miss His blessings. And it is disrespectful to disobey God and miss living in our Promised Land.

Secondly, disobedience causes pain to the one who disobeys. How would you have felt if you wandered for forty years and never entered the Promised Land? It must be a horrible feeling to know God brought you out of bondage, but your sin still caused you to miss His best. Joshua 5:6 says that except for Caleb and Joshua, the older generation didn't even get to see Canaan. They never got to look at what God was leading them to. These men of war never got to live in peace. Because they never stopped fighting against God, they missed the ultimate victory God had for them on earth. While God forgives, sin always

105

has consequences. God is faithful to restore, but disobedience is always painful.

Finally, disobedience also hurts those around us. Sin always has a ripple effect. People closest to you are the ones most affected by your disobedience. Talk to the parents of a prodigal son. Question the relatives of an addict or the child of an alcoholic. Sin hurts and sin causes heartache. Just ask the new generation headed to the Promised Land if their parents' sin negatively impacted their faith journey.

If it were not for the grace of God, where would we be? I am so thankful for God's grace that covers our sins and restores our lives. If you are anything like me, let His grace move you to a place where you live in obedience. As you live in submission to Christ, you display your respect and love for your Father God, while you and those around you enjoy the fullness of all God has planned for you.

As someone once appropriately said, "Sin will take you further than you want to go, keep you longer than you wanted to stay, and cost you more than you want to pay." Disobedience cost one generation of Israel forty years of wandering in the wilderness and the Promised Land.

Questions:

1. How has disobeying God's voice impacted your life?

2. In what ways has your sin influenced others?

3. How does Galatians 6:7-9 relate to today's devotion?

> [7] Do not be deceived: God is not mocked, for whatever one sows, that will he also reap. [8] For the one who sows to his own flesh will from the flesh reap corruption, but the one who sows to the Spirit will from the Spirit reap eternal life. [9] And let us not grow weary of doing good, for in due season we will reap, if we do not give up.

4. How can God heal and restore you by His grace as you seek to faithfully obey Him today?

Day Twenty-Five

Joshua

Breaking Generational Sins

Our laziness after God is our crying sin . . .
No man gets God who does not follow hard after Him.
E.M. Bounds[1]

Text: Joshua 5:7
[7] So it was their children, whom he raised up in their place, that Joshua circumcised. For they were uncircumcised, because they had not been circumcised on the way.

Thoughts:
After years of wandering, Israel should have been ready for war as soon as they crossed over. The flooded river had yielded to the Lord, but the people of God had not surrendered to Him yet! They set up stones to remember Him in chapter 4, but they still hadn't settled some issues in their hearts! They still had two symbols of yielding to settle with God: Circumcision and Passover.

The first symbol was circumcision. The Israelites had been wandering in the wilderness for 40 years. But all the young men born during these years were uncircumcised. Why? One word: disobedience. And why now? This would incapacitate all of their men for days. They would be hurting and healing and would be no help for a war. What is the point of additional pain during this part of the journey? The people of God needed to yield to the commands of God. There is no better way to get ready for our battles than by improving our dedication to God. To conquer our enemies, we need to improve our commitment to God. We desperately need His help if we are going to be victors instead of victims in the battles we face. And God works through those who obey His Word and dedicate themselves to His service.

I love God's grace observed in Joshua 5:7. When one generation disobeyed, God raised up another one in its place. When fathers did not live up to the significance of the sign of their covenant, God circumcised another generation of sons to serve Him in their place.

This gives me great comfort because generational sins concern me. The following Scriptures have always disturbed and alarmed me:

Exodus 20:5 (ESV)

[5] You shall not bow down to them or serve them, for I the Lord your God am a jealous God, visiting the iniquity of the fathers on the children to the third and the fourth generation of those who hate me,

Exodus 34:6-7 (ESV)

[6] The Lord passed before him and proclaimed, "The LORD, the LORD, a God merciful and gracious, slow to anger, and abounding in steadfast love and faithfulness, [7] keeping steadfast love for thousands, forgiving iniquity and transgression and sin, but who will by no means clear the guilty, visiting the iniquity of the fathers on the children and the children's children, to the third and the fourth generation."

Deuteronomy 5:8-10 (ESV)

[8] "'You shall not make for yourself a carved image, or any likeness of anything that is in heaven above, or that is on the earth beneath, or that is in the water under the earth. [9] You shall not bow down to them or serve them; for I the Lord your God am

a jealous God, visiting the iniquity of the fathers on the children to the third and fourth generation of those who hate me, [10] but showing steadfast love to thousands of those who love me and keep my commandments.

God told Israel several times about the sin of one person visiting children down to the third and fourth generation. Does God's Word teach that God punishes my grandchildren for my sin? I believe the true meaning of these warnings from God is as follows: Sin affects other people. When a father indulges in a sinful life, his children are likely to practice the same lifestyle. For example, children of addicts often turn to drugs and alcohol because they watch their parents' bad example. The effects of sin are naturally passed down from one generation to the next. I believe these Scriptures in Exodus and Deuteronomy were a warning from God that children choose to repeat the sins of their fathers.

The Jewish Targum was an Aramaic translation of the Hebrew Old Testament. This ancient document helped Jews to interpret Scripture. This manuscript points out that Exodus 20:5 refers specifically to "ungodly fathers" and "rebellious children." This correlates with Deuteronomy 5:9, which specifies sin affecting "those who hate" God. Deuteronomy 5:10 balances this with the steadfast love shown by God to "those who love" Him and keep His commandments.

There is an increasing trend in our culture to blame sin on a generational curse. It is easier to accuse our fathers than it is to take personal responsibility for our own faults. Yet, God's Word teaches that God shows love to those who love Him. We have the power to overcome the mistakes of our families because we have a God who loves to extend His infinite grace and steadfast love.

At the same time, we need to understand the warning of the serious consequences of a life lived apart from God. God punishes sin and our lifestyle can leave a negative legacy that can cause harm for years to come. The Good News is that there is a cure for the generational curse. In one word, the cure is repentance. If we repent from our sins and turn back to Him, our God can forgive, heal, and restore. May God raise up a generation of disciples who love Him greatly and serve Him faithfully.

Questions:

1. What spiritual legacy are you leaving behind for your children and grandchildren?

2. What needs to take place in your life so that God can raise you up for His service?

Day Twenty-Six

Joshua

Reproach Rolled Away

For the Scripture says,
"Everyone who believes in Him will not be put to shame."
Romans 10:11

Jesus isn't trying to expose you to put shame on you.
He's trying to expose the sin that has its chains around you.
Lysa TerKeurst[1]

Text: Joshua 5:8-9
    [8] When the circumcising of the whole nation was finished, they remained in their places in the camp until they were healed. [9] And the Lord said to Joshua, "Today I have rolled away the reproach of Egypt from you." And so the name of that place is called Gilgal to this day.

Thoughts:
    When the nation of Israel was obedient to keep the sign of the covenant, God "rolled away" the people's reproach. The word used for "reproach" is a Hebrew word "herpah" that means shame or disgrace. While the people of God had been delivered from Egypt geographically, they had wandered in the wilderness for forty years physically and spiritually. Everything God promised Abraham 500 years earlier had been delayed for four decades because of disobedience. The whole nation was disgraced in the eyes of everyone who knew of their plight.

It is enlightening to note other places this word "reproach" is found in Scripture. Genesis 34 records the account of Leah's daughter, Dinah, being violated by a Hivite named Shechem. This great sin of Shechem brought shame and disgrace to Dinah and her family. Genesis 34:14 records these words from Jacob's sons before they avenged her assault and killed Shechem:

> They said to them, "We cannot do this thing, to give our sister to one who is uncircumcised, for that would be a disgrace to us."

The word for disgrace here is the same word found in Joshua 5:9 and is again tied to someone who is uncircumcised. For forty years, the nation of Israel had not kept its covenant with God. Their uncircumcised men were a symbol of their sin and had brought shame on the entire nation.

This word for reproach is also found in Genesis 30:22-23:

> [22] Then God remembered Rachel, and God listened to her and opened her womb. [23] She conceived and bore a son and said, "God has taken away my reproach." [24] And she called his name Joseph, saying, "May the Lord add to me another son!"

Joseph was Jacob's twelfth child, but his first with Rachel. When God allowed Rachel to conceive and give birth to a child, she said, "God has taken away my reproach." Then she named him Joseph which means, "Jehovah shall add." God adds to our lives by taking away our shame. He removes our disgrace and adds His grace.

The Lord told Joshua, "Today I have rolled away the reproach of Egypt from you." And Joshua 5:9 concludes with these words: "And so the name of that place is called Gilgal to this day." The Hebrew for "rolled away" is "galal." It is a play on words with the name "Gilgal." The name "Gilgal" means "a circle of stones." Remember, the Israelites had set up this circle of stones as a memorial of when God brought them across the Jordan on dry ground. Now we see that the memorial would have an even deeper meaning. Every time they looked at the stones or said the word "Gilgal," they would be reminded of the river crossing, yes, but also that God has rolled away their shame. What a great testimony to God's restoration and redemption! And just as He did for the Israelites, He can roll away our shame and give us a fresh start!

Questions:

1. In what specific ways has God removed your shame? Why would you live in guilt over your past when God has the power to roll it away?

2. What is your Gilgal with God?

3. What memorials do you have in your life to remind you of the time that God rolled away your shame?

Day Twenty-Seven

Joshua

Only God!

God's mercy may seem slow, but it is sure.
The Lord in His unfailing wisdom has appointed a time
for the outgoings of His gracious power,
and God's time is the best time.
Charles Spurgeon[1]

Text: Joshua 5:10
[10] While the people of Israel were encamped at Gilgal, they kept the Passover on the fourteenth day of the month in the evening on the plains of Jericho.

Thoughts:
Israel renewed their covenant commitment with God by observing circumcision. Now they could enjoy the Passover celebration.

> If the circumcision was a reminder of who they were, the celebration of the Passover was a reminder of who God was. This was the first time this generation of Hebrews had celebrated the Passover. The Passover celebration acknowledged that they were God's covenant people and it acknowledged that their covenant God was a God of great power.[2]

Joshua 5:10 marks only the third time that the nation of Israel celebrated the Passover. The first Passover was the tenth and final plague that God sent to set His people free. Exodus 12 gives this account. Numbers 9:1-5 records the second Passover celebrated by Israel one year after their departure from Egypt. Our Scripture for today records just the third Passover in a forty-year time period. David Howard notes: "The Passover celebration in Joshua would now mark Israel's entrance into Canaan just as it had earlier marked Israel's exodus from Egypt."[3] The sacrifice of a spotless lamb and the celebration of God's people marked significant moments in the journey of God's people.

The Bible is an incredibly detailed and precise book. Back in Joshua 4:19, we are given the exact day Israel completed their crossing of the Jordan.

> [19] The people came up out of the Jordan on the tenth day of the first month, and they encamped at Gilgal on the east border of Jericho.

The first month of the Jewish calendar was Nisan. Scripture specifically says, "the tenth day of the first month."

Why did God have His people come out of the Jordan River and step foot on their Promised Land on this specific day? To fully understand the answer, you have to look at God's instructions for the Passover in Exodus 12:1-6.

> [1] The Lord said to Moses and Aaron in the land of Egypt, [2] "This month shall be for you the beginning of months. It shall be the first month of the year for you. [3] Tell all the congregation of Israel that on the tenth day of this month every man shall take a lamb according to their fathers' houses, a lamb for a household. [4] And if the household is too small for a lamb, then he and his nearest neighbor shall take according to the number of persons; according to what each can eat you shall make

your count for the lamb. [5] Your lamb shall be without blemish, a male a year old. You may take it from the sheep or from the goats, [6] and you shall keep it until the fourteenth day of this month, when the whole assembly of the congregation of Israel shall kill their lambs at twilight.

To summarize, the lamb was selected on the tenth day. They were to keep the lamb for three days, then sacrifice the lamb and celebrate the Passover on the fourteenth day. Joshua 5:10 specifically notes the date and place of the third Passover: ". . . the fourteenth day of the month in the evening on the plains of Jericho."

Therefore, God's perfect timing was on display when He delivered His people into the Promised Land! This would place Israel in the position to obey the exact instructions for the Passover celebration given in Scripture. And they circumcised the men immediately upon crossing the river, which put them in complete submission to God's Word.

While all those facts are incredible on their own, the greatest aspect of all is what these days point to in the future for God's people. Many scholars believe that on the tenth of Nisan, around AD 32-33, that Jesus made His triumphal entry into Jerusalem. The Lamb of God was chosen before the foundation of the world, but He walked into Jerusalem on the same day Jews were selecting their lambs for Passover. Then on the fourteenth day of Nisan, Jesus was sacrificed at the cross of Calvary!

Only God could put all that together in perfect timing and exact detail to point to His Son's sacrifice for the sins of the world! Only God could orchestrate that precise plan to point to the Lamb of God who takes away the sin of the world.

Questions:

1. What are your thoughts on God's incredible timing?

2. How do the details discussed in today's devotion impact your view of God's greatness? How should they increase your desire to worship Him?

3. In what ways can you celebrate the meaning of Passover in your own spiritual journey?

Day Twenty-Eight

Joshua

Never-Ending Provisions

In the years of living this life of faith,
I have never known God's care to fail.
Brother Andrew[1]

Text: Joshua 5:11-12

¹¹ And the day after the Passover, on that very day, they ate of the produce of the land, unleavened cakes and parched grain. ¹² And the manna ceased the day after they ate of the produce of the land. And there was no longer manna for the people of Israel, but they ate of the fruit of the land of Canaan that year.

Thoughts:

The day after they ate the Passover, Israel ate from the produce of the land. Once the people had God's abundant provisions of the Promised Land, the Lord stopped sending manna. They didn't need the old provisions from God because they had His new provisions.

God always gives us what we need when we need it. He knows us better than we know ourselves. As creator God, He made us. As omniscient God, He knows everything about us. As omnipresent God, He sees us wherever we go. As omnipotent God, there is nothing He can't do. As Jehovah Jireh, He is our provider. His never-ending provisions arise from His divine nature. It is out of who He is that we have the assurance that our Shepherd will guide, guard, and provide.

In God's perfect wisdom, He always provides for our necessities as needs arise. Think about all that God had provided for His people in the wilderness: a cloud by day for shade and a pillar of fire by night for guidance, manna from Heaven daily except the Sabbath, water from a rock, feet that were never swollen, and clothes that never wore out. These are just a few of a long list of God's blessings. And the manna did not cease until they stood among the abundance of the produce of the Promised Land!

In Deuteronomy 8:7-10, God described Canaan as follows:

> ⁷ For the Lord your God is bringing you into a good land, a land of brooks of water, of fountains and springs, flowing out in the valleys and hills, ⁸ a land of wheat and barley, of vines and fig trees and pomegranates, a land of olive trees and honey, ⁹ a land in which you will eat bread without scarcity, in which you will lack nothing, a land whose stones are iron, and out of whose hills you can dig copper. ¹⁰ And you shall eat and be full, and you shall bless the Lord your God for the good land he has given you.

The fields that Israel entered were probably tilled by the people of Jericho. When they heard that Israel had crossed the Jordan River, they fled their fields in fear. They were all locked up inside the city walls of Jericho. The children of Israel simply walked into the harvest of what others had planted and sampled all that God provided for them.

As Deuteronomy 8 described, Israel didn't need manna anymore because they had wheat, barley, figs, pomegranates, and honey. This gives fresh meaning to Psalm 23:5 where David writes, "You prepare a table before me in the presence of my enemies; You anoint my head with oil; my cup overflows."

God surely had prepared Israel a table in the presence of their enemies! Before the walls came down at Jericho, Israel dined in their enemies' fields.

God's provisions are never-ending and multi-faceted. God provided His people with daily sustenance and military victory. He showed His power in the crossing of the Jordan, and He displayed His compassion as He fed His children.

Battles will come for every believer. However, if you obey His commands and surrender to His Lordship, He will provide new provisions for the Promised Land you are entering. As God continues to provide, remember this: Never-ending provisions should result in ceaseless praise.

Questions:

1. God's provision of manna stopped the moment they entered the Promised Land. What does this teach you about God and His provisions?

2. After God told Israel what good things were in store for them in the Promised Land (Deuteronomy 7:10), they received this warning in verses 11-15.

Deuteronomy 8:11-15 (ESV)
[11] "Take care lest you forget the Lord your God by not keeping his commandments and his rules and his statutes, which I command you today, [12] lest, when you have eaten and are full and have built good houses and live in them, [13] and when your herds and flocks multiply and your silver and gold is multiplied and all that you have is multiplied, [14] then your heart be lifted up, and you forget the Lord your God, who brought you out of the land of Egypt, out of the house of slavery, . . .

In what ways have you forgotten God's never-ending provisions? How can you consistently remember all that God has done for you?

Day Twenty-Nine

Joshua

A Divine Encounter

In the case of Abram, three strangers came for dinner.
In the story of Moses, a blazing bush left him wide-eyed and
barefoot. A talking donkey got the attention of Balaam.
A blazing angel guarded the empty tomb of Jesus.
The Bible is famous for surprise encounters.
Yet no visit is more mysterious than this one:
the man with the upraised sword and confident air.
Max Lucado[1]

Text: Joshua 5:13-14a

[13] When Joshua was by Jericho, he lifted up his eyes and looked, and behold, a man was standing before him with his drawn sword in his hand. And Joshua went to him and said to him, "Are you for us, or for our adversaries?" [14] And he said, "No; but I am the commander of the army of the Lord. Now I have come."

Thoughts:

Joshua's encounter recorded in Joshua 5:13-15 has been referred to as a theophany by many students of Scripture. The word "theophany" is a combination of two Greek words that mean "God" and "appearance." A theophany is any visible display of God to human beings that expresses God's character. More specifically, many believe this encounter with Joshua is a Christophany. A Christophany is an appearance of Jesus Christ. One example of a Christophany that is also a theophany is the fourth person in the fiery furnace with Shadrach, Meshach, and Abednego found in Daniel 3:24-25.

Max Lucado, in *Glory Days: Trusting the God Who Fights for You*, shares the following insights on a Christophany:

Do you find this a curious thought? Jesus, BC? Is it difficult to imagine Jesus as an active being before his birth on earth? If so, let me challenge you to widen your imagination. Remember, "Jesus Christ is the same yesterday, today, and forever" (Hebrews 13:8). "He was chosen before the creation of the world" (1 Peter 1:20 NIV). The normal restrictions of time and place do not apply to him. We would be wrong to limit his corporal ministry to thirty-three years in Palestine. Long before Jesus ate with Zacchaeus in Jericho, he shared a moment with Joshua near Jericho.

And what a moment it was. "I am the commander of the army of the Lord," Jesus declared. The human eye saw two armies: the Canaanites and the Israelites. Actually, there was a third. The Lord's army.[2]

When Joshua encounters the presence of God, Scripture says that he approached Him and asked, "Are you for us, or for our adversaries?" This is a great question to a commander from the military leader of the nation of Israel. It is a question any high-ranking soldier would ask. "What is your name, rank, and serial number?" Here is what General Joshua is possibly thinking: "If you are in our army, you are not where you should be. I am the General and I have given no one in my army instructions to be here. If you are with me, you have gone AWOL and need to be disciplined. But if this commander is not on my side, then I need to be ready to fight because you are holding a sword in your hand."

The response Joshua is given is incredible. "No; but I am the commander of the army of the Lord. Now I have come." He tells Joshua, "No." It wasn't a yes or no question. But Joshua will find out in seconds that he is not the one in charge here. The response to Joshua is, "I am not just another soldier, I am the commander of the army of the Lord." The question is not, "Is He on Joshua's side?" The question is "Whose side is Joshua on?" or "Is Joshua with the Lord's army?"

We need a daily reminder that our God fights for us and that the battle is the Lord's. Sometimes we get so busy doing things for God that we forget that God is the One in charge. We need a daily encounter with the living Lord to remind us that we are not the ones calling the shots. Jesus is Lord of Heaven and Earth. This is His world; He just allows us the privilege to live in it. We need to daily align ourselves under His leadership and Lordship because He alone is King of Kings and the Commander of all.

Joshua was headed to Jericho to face impenetrable walls. Before he tackled an impossible task, He needed to remember that He had an all-powerful God. Joshua needed a moment in the presence of the One who would be responsible for victory.

The message to Joshua is unmistakable. *Jericho may have its walls, but, Joshua, you have more. You have God. He is with you.*

Isn't that the word Joshua needed? A reminder of God's mighty presence? Isn't that all any of us need? We need to know that God is near! We are never alone. In our darkest hour, in our deepest questions, the Lord of hosts never leaves us.[3]

Questions:

1. How often do you encounter the presence of God in your life? Jesus is a personal God that wants to reveal Himself to you. If you are not meeting Him regularly, what needs to change in your life to make that your first priority?

2. God can handle any questions that you can bring to Him. He knows what you are struggling with because He is an all-knowing God. So, what questions do you need to take to Him with complete honesty about how you feel?

3. What does it mean to you personally that God wants to speak with you? Jesus is the way, the truth, and the life. (See John 14:6.) How do these attributes encourage you to take all your questions to God?

4. How does God show you His presence before He demonstrates His power?

Day Thirty

Joshua

His Presence Demands Reverence

If true worship is anything, it is a transforming experience.
Warren Wiersbe[1]

Text: Joshua 5:14b-15

[14] …And Joshua fell on his face to the earth and worshiped and said to him, "What does my lord say to his servant?" [15] And the commander of the Lord's army said to Joshua, "Take off your sandals from your feet, for the place where you are standing is holy." And Joshua did so.

Thoughts:

This encounter with Joshua is remarkably like Moses' meeting with God at the burning bush. Joshua and Moses were both standing in the presence of God. They both were told to remove their sandals because they were standing on holy ground. Holy ground moments are transformational situations where God shows up in supernatural ways. His presence demands our reverence. In the same way God instructed Moses to build a tabernacle in the wilderness so He could dwell with His people, our God desires to meet with us. Holy ground is a place for an encounter with the Living God.

In today's Scripture, Joshua asked Him, "What does my Lord say to His servant?" In other words, Joshua said, "What do you want Your servant to do?" When we encounter God's presence, we must not seek His plan over encountering Him personally. Dale Ralph Davis appropriately said,

"... it is more important to recognize God's position than to know God's plans. We can easily become more interested in special guidance than in a right relationship with the Guide."[2]

Joshua had not learned this yet, and the Lord's response to him is revealing. He tells Joshua, "Take off your sandals from your feet, for the place where you are standing is holy." The last few words of verse 15 show us that Joshua listened to the Lord's command.

This moment in God's presence must have had profound effects on Joshua. He had already witnessed God's power many times since the Exodus from Egypt up to the miraculous crossing of the Jordan River. Now, he was encountering God's holiness.

Steven Lawson explains the holiness of God this way:

> First, it has to do with "apart-ness" or "other-ness." The idea of holiness speaks to the profound difference between Him and us. Holiness encompasses His transcendent majesty, and His grand superiority. He is distinctly set apart from us. As one infinitely above us, He alone is worthy of our worship and our adoration. Moses asked: "Who is like You, O Lord, among the gods? Who is like You, majestic in holiness, awesome in glorious deeds, doing wonders?" (Exodus 15:11).
>
> Second, it speaks to His untainted purity, His sinless perfection. God is morally flawless, blameless in all of His ways.[3]

It is impossible to meet with God and leave unchanged. If you ever truly encounter the presence of the Lord, genuine worship is the automatic response. Joshua did what God told him to do because obedience is a form of worship. In our quote for today's devotion, Warren Wiersbe's comment on worship is profound: "If true worship is anything, it is a transforming experience." Worship transforms the worshipper. And true worship demands a response. When God reveals Himself, the reaction is always worship. I searched Scripture and found the following responses of worship: speaking, shouting, singing, kneeling, falling on our face, standing in awe, dancing, clapping, lifting hands, etc. These are just a small sample of ways we respond to God in worship. God's presence always commands a response.

True worship doesn't have a trace of selfishness. True worship is simply giving God the worth due His name. Genuine worship is completely God-centered. When we worship God simply because He is worthy, our motives are pure. This type of worship leaves no place for pride as we respond in humility to all that He is. His appearance creates our awe. God's presence produces pure praise. His holiness causes our humility.

Questions:

1. How is your worship with God? When was the last time you took off your shoes in personal worship because you knew you were standing on holy ground?

2. In what ways do you miss His person because you are too focused on His plan or will for your life? How can you focus more on who He is in your quiet time?

3. What is your Commander telling you to do in your walk with Him? What actions do you need to take so that your response will be like Joshua's?

4. Spend some time allowing the following Scripture to draw you into His presence. Respond by worshipping Him for who He is.

Psalm 86:12-13, 15 (ESV)
    [12] I give thanks to you, O Lord my God, with my whole heart, and I will glorify your name forever. [13] For great is your steadfast love toward me; you have delivered my soul from the depths of Sheol . . . [15] But you, O Lord, are a God merciful and gracious, slow to anger and abounding in steadfast love and faithfulness.

Day Thirty-One

Joshua

The Walls of Jericho

Few Bible stories do more to capture one's imagination than
the story about Joshua and the battle of Jericho. It's the stuff
of Hebrew liturgy that has brought enormous encouragement
to devout Jews down through the centuries. . .
In one way, this is a strange story about an ancient battle.
In another way, it is the model for victorious Christian living.
John Huffman Jr., and Lloyd J. Ogivie[1]

Text: Joshua 6:1-2
   ¹ Now Jericho was shut up inside and outside because of
the people of Israel. None went out, and none came in. ² And
the Lord said to Joshua, "See, I have given Jericho into your
hand, with its king and mighty men of valor."

Thoughts:
   The text today begins with a description of Jericho as "shut
up inside and outside." The people of Jericho were hiding in fear
behind the massive walls of their city. Archeological evidence
has revealed that Jericho was surrounded by a stone wall that
was possibly 40 feet high and 6 feet in thickness. This city was
known for walls that were impassable. Max Lucado eloquently
describes the situation as follows:

   Here is what you need to know about the walls of
   Jericho. They were immense. They wrapped around the
   city like a suit of armor, two concentric circles of stone

133

rising high above the ground. Impenetrable.

Here is what you need to know about Jericho's inhabitants. They were ferocious and barbaric. They withstood all sieges and repelled all invaders. They were guilty of child sacrifice. "They even burn their sons and daughters as sacrifices to their gods!" (Deut. 12:31 NCV). They were a Bronze-age version of the gestapo, ruthless tyrants on the plains of Canaan.[2]

To say that conquering Jericho was no small task would be the understatement of the century. Joshua would face the enormous assignment of defeating Jericho as the first battle after crossing into the Promised Land.

Imagine how Joshua must have felt when He heard God's words in Joshua 6:2: "See, I have given Jericho into your hand, with its king and mighty men of valor." God had already placed the victory over Jericho into Joshua's hands. It was such a done deal that God said it in past tense. "The victory is yours, Joshua. I have assured you success. Just go follow my instructions and you will see the battle has already been won."

The battle for Jericho was really a spiritual battle and would be won by faith in God's power and grace. The plan, the timing, and the results were part of God's meticulous design. . . The real battle with Jericho was not with the Canaanites but with the Israelites, not with the wall of a city but with human hearts.[3]

As we will see in the next few devotions, God's battle strategy was absurd. The real battle would be won or lost depending on whether Israel's faith conquered their fears. Would they trust God enough to obey whatever He told them to do? Would Joshua lead the nation to have faith over their feelings? Every faith decision requires a trust in God that eventually triumphs over our fears. As the nation of Israel discovered, every step around Jericho would also be spiritual steps of faith.

Questions:

1. What walls need to come down in your life in order for you to see God's victory?

2. How difficult is it for you to trust God's power for victory over your own strength for the battle? How can trusting in His promises keep you centered in your approach to difficult circumstances?

3. What present fears are hindering your next steps of faith?

Day Thirty-Two

Joshua

Strange Battle Plans

It is always a test of patience to have to do something
over and over before anything happens.
John G. Butler[1]

Text: Joshua 6:3-5

³ You shall march around the city, all the men of war going around the city once. Thus shall you do for six days. ⁴ Seven priests shall bear seven trumpets of rams' horns before the ark. On the seventh day you shall march around the city seven times, and the priests shall blow the trumpets. ⁵ And when they make a long blast with the ram's horn, when you hear the sound of the trumpet, then all the people shall shout with a great shout, and the wall of the city will fall down flat, and the people shall go up, everyone straight before him."

Thoughts:

The battle of Jericho is unique in so many ways. In fact, God's instructions to Joshua may be stranger here than anywhere else in Scripture. That is a grandiose statement when you consider: a donkey speaking to Balaam (Numbers 22), Jonah swallowed by a large fish and spit up on dry ground (Jonah 2), Elisha leading a group of blind Syrians into Samaria (2 Kings 6). And the list could go on and on. God works in mysterious ways to test our trust and our patience.

Let's look at several facts that are out of place biblically in the battle of Jericho. First, priests led the military march, and they were biblically exempt from fighting. A priest was strictly forbidden to touch a dead person, or he would make himself unclean. (See Leviticus 21:10-11.) Yet in the battle of Jericho, the priests were leading the army in the march around the city.

Second, the ark of the covenant was not normally taken into battle. The ark of the covenant had special instructions because of how sacred a symbol this was for God's people. (See Exodus 25.) The ark represented the actual presence of God. It had to be carried on poles and could not be taken lightly. In fact, two sons of a priest will try to take the ark of the covenant into battle against the Philistines in 1 Samuel 4 and face extreme consequences.

A third unique factor of this battle of Jericho is the use of ram's horns. God had instructed Israel to use silver trumpets for war. This is described in Numbers 10:

> [1] The Lord spoke to Moses, saying, [2] "Make two silver trumpets. Of hammered work you shall make them, and you shall use them for summoning the congregation and for breaking camp. . . [8] The trumpets shall be to you for a perpetual statute throughout your generations. [9] And when you go to war in your land against the adversary who oppresses you, then you shall sound an alarm with the trumpets, that you may be remembered before the Lord your God, and you shall be saved from your enemies."

So, rather than use the usual silver trumpets, God told Joshua to have the priests carry seven trumpets of ram's horns. These trumpets were also known as shofars. The ram's horn was a cherished symbol of God's provision dating back to God's promise to Abraham. In Genesis 22, when Abraham was told to offer Isaac as a sacrifice, God provided a ram in the bush instead.

From that moment on, a ram's horn became a special picture of God's goodness. The ram's horn would be blown to gather a solemn assembly, announce the coronation of a king, and to mark the beginning and ending of a sabbath.

A fourth unique factor of the battle of Jericho is the days of marching. The Israelites marched around Jericho one time a day for six days. The seventh day, they marched around Jericho seven times. Thus, Israel marched around Jericho a total of thirteen times. Since they marched for seven days, one of those seven days had to be the Sabbath. God commanded rest for the Sabbath. Both Exodus 16:29 and Numbers 35:5 state that Jews were only permitted to travel three-quarters of a mile on the Sabbath. So, they broke God's law for the Sabbath to march around Jericho. Actually, some people believe that the seventh day was their Sabbath and they walked around it seven times.

Another distinct characteristic of this battle revolves around the number seven. Seven is a biblical number representing completeness. Seven priests were to carry seven trumpets, walk around Jericho seven days, and on the seventh day they were to walk around it seven times. That is a lot of sevens! God's power brought a complete victory at Jericho.

A final unique factor of this battle was the silence of the army of Israel. We will get more into their silence in tomorrow's devotion. However, for seven days and thirteen trips around Jericho, they could not utter a word.

God was definitely up to something unusual when He sent Joshua and the nation of Israel to defeat Jericho. God often does things in peculiar ways so that people will know that only God can bring the victory. These strange plans also cause His children to act in total trust and surrender to His will.

When my father told me to do something that I thought was absurd, I would always ask, "Why?" His answer was always the same. "Because I said so." Our Heavenly Father gives us commands to test our trust in Him. God wants to know if we will take Him at His Word and follow His will, whatever that word or will may be.

Questions:

1. In what ways do you question God before you obey Him?

2. How does the uniqueness of God's plan lead you to a stronger dependence on Him?

3. Are there any other areas that stand out to you in the battle of Jericho that seem strange and unusual? What are they? Why do you think God chose this plan for defeating Jericho?

Day Thirty-Three

Joshua

Obedience in His Presence

*Obedient action in response to divinely-given promises
is the channel by which the sovereign grace of their covenant
Lord is experienced in the lives of His people.*
David Jackman[1]

Text: Joshua 6:6-7

⁶ So Joshua the son of Nun called the priests and said to them, "Take up the ark of the covenant and let seven priests bear seven trumpets of rams' horns before the ark of the Lord." ⁷ And he said to the people, "Go forward. March around the city and let the armed men pass on before the ark of the Lord."

Thoughts:

The ark of the covenant is mentioned at least ten times in Joshua 6. See if you can get this picture in your mind. The ark of the covenant had seven priests marching in front of it. Each priest was carrying a ram's horn. The armed men of the nation of Israel were to pass before the ark of the Lord as they went forward. There was also a rear guard following the ark. Scripture paints a picture of the army guarding the ark as it moved while the priests sound their trumpets of rams' horns in front of it. There was a huge emphasis on the ark as it circled the walls of Jericho thirteen times over seven days.

I can only imagine what that must have been like from Israel's vantage point. Everyone from priests to soldiers was focused on the representation of God's holy presence. Trumpets were sounded as reminders of God's provision and power. While they were marching around huge walls of intimidation, they were focused on the size of Yahweh God. While they passed walls that were motionless, they focused on the God who moves in power.

Next, imagine what the people in Jericho witnessed. From their towers, their army watched in terror as Israel marched around their city. They would undoubtedly witness Israel's focus on the ark of the covenant. The silence of the army would be haunting to their ears. The sounds of the rams' horns would be ringing, and their hearts would be reeling. Seven days of panic, fear, and stomachs in knots as they waited to see what Israel's God would do. They had known of the crossing of the Jordan River. They certainly had heard the story of the Red Sea parting and the demise of the Egyptians. If the two and a half million people didn't cause overwhelming fear in their hearts, the thoughts of God's power surely did!

Military strategists would tell you that this battle plan was incredibly unwise. They would tell you that the people would be placed in extreme danger as they would be vulnerable to attacks from Jericho's walls. The priests would be sitting ducks as targets. Their trumpets would not serve them well as weapons. While this was not a smart military operation, it was superb spiritually. Nothing could encourage and motivate the children of Israel more than walking in the presence of God for seven days. The strangeness of the battle plan would increase Israel's trust in God. Obedience in His presence leads to victory from His power.

Questions:

1. In what ways do you see God growing your faith spiritually? Are there trials that have come your way that you now perceive as tests of faith?

2. When God asks you to do something unusual, what is your first response? Considering Jericho, what should your response be?

3. How can you creatively put yourself into Scripture to give you more biblical vision and insight to apply God's Word to your daily life?

Day Thiry-Four

Joshua

A Lesson from Silence

Whoever is slow to anger is better than the mighty,
and he who rules his spirit than he who takes a city.
Proverbs 16:32

Text: Joshua 6:8-11

[8] And just as Joshua had commanded the people, the seven priests bearing the seven trumpets of rams' horns before the Lord went forward, blowing the trumpets, with the ark of the covenant of the Lord following them. [9] The armed men were walking before the priests who were blowing the trumpets, and the rear guard was walking after the ark, while the trumpets blew continually. [10] But Joshua commanded the people, "You shall not shout or make your voice heard, neither shall any word go out of your mouth, until the day I tell you to shout. Then you shall shout." [11] So he caused the ark of the Lord to circle the city, going about it once. And they came into the camp and spent the night in the camp.

Thoughts:

Walking around the fortified city of Jericho thirteen times in six days would have been challenging all by itself. However, Joshua gave the people a very difficult assignment within an extremely unusual plan. We read in Joshua 6:10 that Joshua commanded the people, "You shall not shout or make your voice heard, neither shall any word go out of your mouth until the day I tell you to shout."

Their silence was commanded in three parts. First, they were told not to shout. The Hebrew for shout is "rua" and means "to raise a shout." It was a word commonly used in the Old Testament to describe a war cry or shout of alarm. This is the same word recorded in 1 Samuel 17:52 used to describe the shout from Israel when David defeated Goliath:

> [52] And the men of Israel and Judah rose with a shout and pursued the Philistines as far as Gath and the gates of Ekron, so that the wounded Philistines fell on the way from Shaaraim as far as Gath and Ekron.

This word for shout was also commonly found in the Psalms to describe praise. When used in this context, the word conveys the meaning, "to raise a glad cry." An example of this use of the word is found in Psalm 95:1-2:

> [1] Oh come, let us sing to the Lord; let us make a joyful noise to the rock of our salvation! [2] Let us come into His presence with thanksgiving; let us make a joyful noise to Him with songs of praise!

The people of Israel had to refrain from any war cry during these thirteen marches around Jericho. They could not even raise a glad cry. They were to remain silent.

The second part of Joshua's command of silence was they couldn't make their voice heard. This meant that they were not to even utter a sound. The third part of their strict orders was, "neither shall any word go out of your mouth." They couldn't say a word nor make a sound. This three-fold instruction stressed complete and utter silence for the duration of their Jericho trips. Thus, the only sound coming from the nation of Israel would be from the rams' horns.

This was a huge lesson in silence. David would write about silence in Psalm 62:1-2, 5-7:

> **1** For God alone my soul waits in silence; from Him comes my salvation. **2** He alone is my rock and my salvation, my fortress; I shall not be greatly shaken.
> . . . **5** For God alone, O my soul, wait in silence, for my hope is from Him. **6** He only is my rock and my salvation, my fortress; I shall not be shaken. **7** On God rests my salvation and my glory; my mighty rock, my refuge is God.

The word for "silence" here in Psalm 61 means "a quiet waiting." It can also be translated, "to lay at rest." Sometimes we talk too much and don't take time to listen to God. Obviously, God wants us to bring our requests before Him. He desires honest confession and inhabits the praise of His people. Yet there are times for silence when we need to be still and know that He is God. We desperately need times of silence where we consider the glory of His greatness.

The nation of Israel had thirteen quiet laps around Jericho. That is a lot of steps in silence. As they listened to the trumpet blasts from the shofars, they could focus on God's provisions and His power. They had plenty of time to reflect on His goodness and their inadequacies. They had to realize that it was impossible for them to take Jericho if God did not intervene. They had a week of contemplative worship. After six and half days of silence, Joshua 6:10 ends with these words: "Then you shall shout." Imagine how loud they shouted after a week of complete silence! Maybe our silence before the Lord could lead to louder praise.

Questions:

1. How are your moments of silence with the Lord? What needs to happen in your relationship with God for you to become a better listener?

2. Read Psalm 46:7-10 below. Then take some moments of silence and know that He is God.

> ⁷ The Lord of hosts is with us;
> the God of Jacob is our fortress. *Selah*
> ⁸ Come, behold the works of the Lord,
> how He has brought desolations on the earth.
> ⁹ He makes wars cease to the end of the earth;
> He breaks the bow and shatters the spear;
> He burns the chariots with fire.
> ¹⁰ "Be still, and know that I am God.
> I will be exalted among the nations,
> I will be exalted in the earth!"

Day Thirty-Five

Joshua

Total Surrender to His Ways

> [8] For my thoughts are not your thoughts,
> neither are your ways my ways, declares the Lord.
> [9] For as the heavens are higher than the earth,
> · so are my ways higher than your ways
> and my thoughts than your thoughts.
> **Isaiah 55:8-9**

> "As promised deliverances must be expected in God's way,
> so they must be expected in his time."
> **Matthew Henry**[1]

Text: Joshua 6:12-14

[12] Then Joshua rose early in the morning, and the priests took up the ark of the Lord. [13] And the seven priests bearing the seven trumpets of rams' horns before the ark of the Lord walked on, and they blew the trumpets continually. And the armed men were walking before them, and the rear guard was walking after the ark of the Lord, while the trumpets blew continually. [14] And the second day they marched around the city once, and returned into the camp. So they did for six days.

Thoughts:

When you yield to God, it requires total surrender. This means that God doesn't do it your way. He does it His way. You have heard it said, "God works in mysterious ways." Don't miss

147

the meaning behind mysterious ways. He works in ways where only He gets the glory.

Often we miss the miraculous because we pick our predictable plan over His mysterious method. There is no miracle needed if you can do it in your power! We place our faith in a God who can turn our impossible situation into His next miracle. The battle of Jericho, recorded in Joshua 6, is another example of His miraculous power.

This miracle of the Jericho walls coming down begins with a commitment to God's divine plan. The armed men were to march around the city once a day for six days. Then on the seventh day, they were to march around it seven times. After the seventh time on the seventh day, the priests were to blow their trumpets. All the people were to then shout and then the walls were to come tumbling down. What a plan!

The purpose of this plan wasn't to impress the Canaanites but to teach the Israelites. God made them walk around those walls to convince them that there was no hope of conquering Jericho by human strength or strategy. He wanted the Israelites to know that they had no hope except in their Commander of the army of the Lord. Their total trust had to be in His power.

You may be going through a battle in your life that seems completely hopeless. Perhaps you feel that you are marching around the walls of Jericho, again and again. It seems like you are accomplishing nothing, and you are wondering if there is any point in going on. Maybe God is trying to teach you the same lesson He taught the Israelites. He wants you to understand that your only hope is in Him. He may be waiting for you to admit that this "Jericho" in your life is too powerful for you. But no enemy is too powerful for God. No wall is so strong that He can't level it with just a shout! No wall is too high that He can't bring it down with just a Hallelujah! He is waiting for you to turn to Him and say, "I trust You to topple these walls. I can do nothing in my own strength. My only hope is in You."

And that total trust in Him must be displayed when everything He is telling you to do seems so irrational. Try to view the situation as a soldier in Israel's army. What would you be thinking when you heard the plan for battle? There are going to be challenges that God calls you to perform that will probably seem every bit as irrational. You can't understand why God would choose to do it this way. Why has God placed you in a job you hate, with a boss who mistreats you, with coworkers who are cruel to you? Why has God placed you in a classroom with an atheist professor who daily ridicules your faith? Why is your family so dysfunctional, and why should you stay committed to people who don't seem to care? Why has God allowed your business or ministry to fail? Didn't He promise you a victorious life? Why must you walk around this problem for days? Sometimes His plan for your life seems to make no sense.

God said, "Do it this way," and Joshua did it. Joshua put His trust in God's wisdom, not human reasoning. He obeyed his Commander. And the walls came down! Put your trust in His power and plan. And don't forget to give Him all the credit when the walls come crashing down. When He sends down the solution to your problem, make sure the shouts of praise go back up to Him.

Questions:

1. What areas of your situation seem the most hopeless?

2. Why is total surrender to His ways so difficult?

3. What is God telling you to do right now in your situation?

4. What attributes of God can you focus on to give you complete confidence in His power over your problem?

Day Thirty-Six

Joshua

Walls Fall as Faith Rises

³⁰ By faith the walls of Jericho fell down after they had been encircled for seven days. ³¹ By faith Rahab the prostitute did not perish with those who were disobedient, because she had given a friendly welcome to the spies.
Hebrews 11:30-31

Text: Joshua 6:15-21

¹⁵ On the seventh day they rose early, at the dawn of day, and marched around the city in the same manner seven times. It was only on that day that they marched around the city seven times. ¹⁶ And at the seventh time, when the priests had blown the trumpets, Joshua said to the people, "Shout, for the Lord has given you the city. ¹⁷ And the city and all that is within it shall be devoted to the Lord for destruction. Only Rahab the prostitute and all who are with her in her house shall live, because she hid the messengers whom we sent. ¹⁸ But you, keep yourselves from the things devoted to destruction, lest when you have devoted them you take any of the devoted things and make the camp of Israel a thing for destruction and bring trouble upon it. ¹⁹ But all silver and gold, and every vessel of bronze and iron, are holy to the Lord; they shall go into the treasury of the Lord." ²⁰ So the people shouted, and the trumpets were blown. As soon as the people heard the sound of the trumpet, the people shouted a great shout, and the wall fell down flat, so that the people went up into the city, every man straight before him, and they captured

the city. [21] Then they devoted all in the city to destruction, both men and women, young and old, oxen, sheep, and donkeys, with the edge of the sword.

Thoughts:

After days of complete silence, God's people give a collective shout! And after a week of marching in faith, God tears down the walls of Jericho! This was one of the greatest victories in the history of the nation of Israel and the first conquest in their long-awaited Promised Land. There would be many more victories in their land of promise, but Jericho would always be the inaugural one on their journey of faith.

The New Testament would later draw our attention to this encounter by including it in the Hall of Fame of Faith. The writer of Hebrews lets us know that God worked His power through the faith of His people. The walls of Jericho fell "by faith," "after they had been encircled for seven days." The Israelites' faith stood for seven days before the walls fell. They trusted God enough to obey God's unfathomable battle plan for a week. Every time they circled Jericho, their faith grew stronger. Their long period of silence gave them time to listen to God, so He could strengthen their faith. They were walking in circles physically, but they were moving forward in faith.

Our Scripture for today's devotion highlights the culmination of Israel's faith. It also emphasizes the faith of Rahab as we will discuss more in tomorrow's devotion. While they all waited for God's timing, their trust in God grew stronger. Both Israel and Rahab learned to trust God faithfully and obey Him fully.

Across time, God has asked His people to trust and obey Him completely, especially when they can't yet fully see His plans. In 1866, D. L. Moody led a series of meetings in Brockton, Massachusetts. Daniel B. Towner, director of the music department at Moody Bible Institute was leading the music during those assemblies. Towner gave the following account of what happened:

> One night a young man rose in a testimony meeting and said, "I am not quite sure—but I am going to trust, and I am going to obey." I just jotted that sentence down and sent it with the little story to the Rev. J. H. Sammis, a Presbyterian minister.[1]

From there, Sammis wrote the great hymn, "Trust and Obey":

> When we walk with the Lord, In the light of His Word
> What a glory He sheds on our way.
> While we do His good will, He abides with us still,
> And with all who will trust and obey.
> Trust and obey, for there's no other way,
> To be happy in Jesus, but to trust and obey.[2]

Every Christian has a Jericho to overcome, and a Promise Land to claim. We all have walls in our lives that could keep us from experiencing God's best. It may be the wall of a habit you can't seem to defeat. It may be the wall of unforgiveness, bitterness, hate, jealousy, gossip, or slander. It may be the wall of pornography, prejudice, or pride.

Whatever our Jericho may be, only the Lord Jesus can cause those walls to come tumbling down. God may ask something of us that we did not expect nor understand, but if we want to go to Canaan, and "be happy in Jesus," then we better learn to "Trust and Obey!"

Questions:

1. How is your faith being tested and in what ways is it growing stronger in the Lord?

2. How is waiting difficult but, at the same time, essential to your faith growing deeper?

3. Is there anything about your faith in God that would place it in the Hall of Fame in Hebrews 11? Why or why not?

4. What are your thoughts on these words from the song "Trust and Obey"?

> Trust and obey, for there's no other way,
> To be happy in Jesus, but to trust and obey.

Day Thirty-Seven

Joshua

Saved Alive

Through salvation our past has been forgiven,
our present is given meaning,
and our future is secure.
Rick Warren[1]

Text: Joshua 6:22-25

²² But to the two men who had spied out the land, Joshua said, "Go into the prostitute's house and bring out from there the woman and all who belong to her, as you swore to her." ²³ So the young men who had been spies went in and brought out Rahab and her father and mother and brothers and all who belonged to her. And they brought all her relatives and put them outside the camp of Israel. ²⁴ And they burned the city with fire, and everything in it. Only the silver and gold, and the vessels of bronze and of iron, they put into the treasury of the house of the Lord. ²⁵ But Rahab the prostitute and her father's household and all who belonged to her, Joshua saved alive. And she has lived in Israel to this day, because she hid the messengers whom Joshua sent to spy out Jericho.

Thoughts:

There is a book and a movie with the simple but riveting title "Alive!" The book was published in 1974 and the movie was released in 1993. They both tell the same incredible story that began on Friday, October 13, 1972. On that fatal day, a Uruguayan rugby team was traveling on Air Force Flight 571

155

and crashed in the Andes Mountains. Of the 45 people on board, only 16 people would survive this horrific event. Rescue teams searched for eight days for survivors but were forced to terminate their search. The survivors were left on their own in sub-freezing temperatures for 72 days, resorting to extreme measures to stay alive. They fought exposure to the intense cold, starvation, and an avalanche. Three of the survivors left the group and hiked for ten days. On the tenth day, they came across three men on horseback that would eventually lead to the rescue of all sixteen survivors. On December 23, 1972, they were saved. People called it the "Miracle in the Andes." The headlines of several news outlets shared about the incredible rescue with the words "Found alive."[2]

Rahab's story is another true story of salvation and rescue. After the walls of Jericho fell, Rahab and her family were found alive.

There is a subtle hint to the magnitude of this miracle found back in Joshua 6:20.

> [20] So the people shouted, and the trumpets were blown. As soon as the people heard the sound of the trumpet, the people shouted a great shout, and the wall fell down flat, so that the people went up into the city, every man straight before him, and they captured the city.

Did you catch the phrase, ". . . and the wall fell down flat"? The original language for "fell down flat" consists of two Hebrew words. One is the verb "naphal" which means "to fall upon." It is the same word used in Genesis 2:21 when Scripture says, "God caused a deep sleep to fall upon Adam." The other Hebrew word is the adjective "gadol," which means, "exceedingly great, severe, and violent." So the walls of Jericho fell violently with great severity.

However, in this mess of debris was a miracle of deliverance. The walls violently fell, but Rahab and her family were victoriously saved. In the midst of death all around them, they were "saved alive." Our God rescues and saves! He is the deliverer who brings life out of death and triumph out of tragedy!

Archeologists have excavated the Jericho site, and their findings match everything Joshua 6 reports on the fall of Jericho.

> Surrounding the entire city was an enormous earthen embankment with huge, stone retaining walls at its base. At the top of the embankment stood a colossal, 46-foot-high mud-brick wall. The houses were built on those massive, thick walls.
>
> Extraordinary archaeological discoveries have been made at Jericho. The Bible says the walls "fell down flat" (6:20). Piles of mud bricks from the collapsed wall were found in 1997, confirming the walls were not destroyed by a battering ram, but that they collapsed. The Bible also says the entire city and everything in it was burned (v. 24). A layer of ash three feet thick with remnants of burnt timbers and debris was found.
>
> However, the most fascinating discovery was on the north side of the city. The wall and houses built against it were preserved.[3]

God made good on His promise to save Rahab. The scarlet thread was the symbol for the warriors of Israel, but she and her family were saved by God alone.

Questions:

1. How do you think Rahab felt when she heard the walls of Jericho coming down? What do you think her reaction was when she was "saved alive"?

2. Read the following Scriptures and spend some time today praising God for the salvation only He can bring.

Ephesians 2:4-5 (ESV)
⁴ But God, being rich in mercy, because of the great love with which he loved us, ⁵ even when we were dead in our trespasses, made us alive together with Christ – by grace you have been saved . . .

Acts 16:31 (ESV)
And they said, "Believe in the Lord Jesus, and you will be saved, you and your household."

Day Thirty-Eight

Joshua
___

God's Favor and Forewarning

Public victories are the results
of private visits with the Lord.
Skip Heitzig[1]

Text: Joshua 6:26-27

[26] Joshua laid an oath on them at that time, saying, "Cursed before the Lord be the man who rises up and rebuilds this city, Jericho. "At the cost of his firstborn shall he lay its foundation, and at the cost of his youngest son shall he set up its gates." [27] So the Lord was with Joshua, and his fame was in all the land.

Thoughts:

Joshua gave an oath that placed a curse on anyone who tried to rebuild Jericho. Joshua 6:26 gives the consequences with these words, "At the cost of his firstborn shall he lay its foundation, and at the cost of his youngest son shall he set up its gates." About 530 years after the walls of Jericho came down, someone attempted to rebuild the city. It happened during the reign of King Ahab and was attempted by a man named Hiel from Bethel. 1 Kings 16:33-34 tells the account:

[33] . . . Ahab did more to provoke the Lord, the God of Israel, to anger than all the kings of Israel who were before him. [34] In his days Hiel of Bethel built Jericho. He laid its foundation at the cost of Abiram his firstborn, and

159

set up its gates at the cost of his youngest son Segub, according to the word of the Lord, which he spoke by Joshua the son of Nun.

Hiel lost his sons because he didn't listen to the warning from God. It happened just as Joshua said it would!

The account of Jericho closes with these words in Joshua 6:27, "So the Lord was with Joshua, and his fame was in all the land." The word "fame" in this verse is the Hebrew word, "shoma." It can be used to refer to "fame" or "a report." It is only found four times in the Old Testament. Of those four, two are in reference to Joshua. (See also Joshua 9:9.) This word is used once in reference to Mordecai in Esther 9:4 and again in Jeremiah 6:24 to describe the prophetic report of the invasion of the land of Judah and the siege of Jerusalem by the Chaldean army. Joshua was famous and the report of what God was doing was all over Canaan.

However, the only reason Joshua was famous was because the Lord was with him. Joshua was an obedient servant and a courageous leader, but God was the one who won every battle and defeated every foe.

God told Joshua, from the beginning of his leadership, that He would be with him. Remember what God said to Joshua back in Joshua 1:5 and 1:9:

> ⁵ "No man shall be able to stand before you all the days of your life. Just as I was with Moses, so I will be with you. I will not leave you or forsake you. . .
>
> ⁹ Have I not commanded you? Be strong and courageous. Do not be frightened, and do not be dismayed, for the Lord your God is with you wherever you go."

God always keeps His promises. He kept them in reference to always being with Joshua, and He kept them with regards to Jericho. If God says it, that settles it. God's favor and His forewarnings are undeniable.

Questions:

1. Why do you think God cursed anyone who would seek to rebuild Jericho?

2. How do you know that the Lord is with you?

3. Because the Lord was with Joshua, the "fame" or "report" of Joshua and the Israelites was spread throughout the land. What "report" of you would your friends and neighbors receive today based on your relationship with God?

Day Thirty-Nine

Joshua

The Roller Coaster of Faith

We must learn from this that God takes sin seriously,
even if we do not, and that sin is the real cause
of defeat for God's people.
James Montgomery Boice[1]

Text: Joshua 7:1
[1] But the people of Israel broke faith in regard to the devoted things, for Achan the son of Carmi, son of Zabdi, son of Zerah, of the tribe of Judah, took some of the devoted things. And the anger of the Lord burned against the people of Israel.

Thoughts:
You would think that after what God did at Jericho, everybody would be trusting Him. You would expect that the chapter after Jericho would be another miracle, another victory, another moment where God showed up and showed out. Instead, there is the story of how God's people were betrayed from within and ambushed from without.

How much tragedy can one traitor bring about? Just ask one spouse who has been betrayed. Question one family who has been deceived. Ask one company who has faced embezzlement from within. Inquire of one special forces unit that found a spy within its ranks! How much harm can one traitor cause? He can bring defeat to his entire nation.

Today's reading introduces what must be the saddest section in the book of Joshua. The nation has just entered the

Promised Land. They have finally arrived. They crossed the Jordan at flood stage. They saw God bring down the walls of Jericho with a shout! But right after celebration comes setback. We will discover in our study that the cause is deeper than just the moral and spiritual weakness of one man. God will hold the entire nation responsible.

The center point of this sad story revolved around a man named Achan. And his actions bring defeat for his own nation, the lives of thirty-six Israelite soldiers, the death of his entire family, and the loss of his own life. Innocent people died and the battle was lost because of the hidden sins of one man!

Please understand that the seeds of Israel's defeat at Ai were planted at the very moment of Israel's triumph over Jericho. Take note of the fact that your sin doesn't just affect you. As we will see more clearly in future readings, it is not only Achan that will pay for his sin. Achan's children, his family, and his nation will all pay a high price for his greed. I beg you to see your sin as God sees it! Repent before it is too late! Defeat does not have to be the end of your story.

Notice that Joshua 7 begins with these words: "But the people of Israel broke faith in regard to the devoted things. . ." The Old Testament word for "broke faith" is a word that literally means, "a very unfaithful act," "a trespass," or "treachery". Sin is a violation of God's law and treason against our Lord and Savior. Achan had stolen silver and gold. He had also stolen a Canaanite garment. God had said to destroy these items. Instead, Achan coveted and took them.

Joshua 7:1 closes with words that no one ever wants to hear said about them personally or their nation corporately: "And the anger of the Lord burned against the people of Israel." The Hebrew word for anger here is "aph" and is pronounced "af." This is a very interesting word in the language of the Old Testament.

It can be translated as follows: "a nostril, nose, face, or anger." It is the same word translated as "nostrils" in Genesis 2:7.

> [7] then the Lord God formed the man of dust from the ground and breathed into his nostrils the breath of life, and the man became a living creature.

It is the word "wrath" found in Psalm 2:5-6 and "anger" in Psalm 7:6:

> [2:5] Then he will speak to them in his wrath, and terrify them in his fury, saying, [6] "As for me, I have set my King on Zion, my holy hill."

> [7:6] Arise, O Lord, in your anger; lift yourself up against the fury of my enemies; awake for me; you have appointed a judgment.

Have you ever been so angry that your nostrils flared? When you have intense anger, your face shows it. God was so angry with the sin of Achan and the Israelites that you could see it on His face! You are in trouble when God flares His nostrils. David described this type of anger from God in Psalm 18:7-8:

> [7] Then the earth reeled and rocked; the foundations also of the mountains trembled and quaked, because he was angry. [8] Smoke went up from his nostrils, and devouring fire from his mouth; glowing coals flamed forth from him.

May we live in such a way to never see this look on His face!

Questions:

1. How are you tempted more after spiritual victories?

2. In what areas of your life have you ". . . broke[n] faith in regard to devoted things"?

3. What would be your response if you knew that God's anger burned against you?

Day Forty

Joshua

The Danger of Fighting Your Battles Alone

Do not grow overconfident following a few victories.
Should you not rely upon the Holy Spirit you will soon be
thrown once more into a distressing experience.
With holy diligence, you must cultivate
an attitude of dependency.
Watchman Nee[1]

Text: Joshua 7:2-5

² Joshua sent men from Jericho to Ai, which is near Beth-aven, east of Bethel, and said to them, "Go up and spy out the land." And the men went up and spied out Ai. ³ And they returned to Joshua and said to him, "Do not have all the people go up, but let about two or three thousand men go up and attack Ai. Do not make the whole people toil up there, for they are few." ⁴ So about three thousand men went up there from the people. And they fled before the men of Ai, ⁵ and the men of Ai killed about thirty-six of their men and chased them before the gate as far as Shebarim and struck them at the descent. And the hearts of the people melted and became as water.

Thoughts:

There were several factors that led to Israel's defeat at Ai. Future verses from this chapter will reveal Achan's sin, but Israel and Joshua were not completely innocent in this matter.

The first step towards defeat was a lack of prayer. Before Jericho, Joshua was literally in the presence of God and fell on his knees in worship. Before the walls came down, Joshua had spent time in the presence of the Lord. He had inquired of the Lord and received specific instructions. Nowhere in the account of Ai do we find Joshua or the leadership asking God for guidance. There is no prayer or praise lifted up to God. There is no holy ground moment before the battle. There is no silent time to hear God speak. Joshua sends men to spy out the land. The men return with their opinions on the matter. However, no one stopped to get God's opinion. They were acting in their own strength and were not trusting in God for anything concerning this battle. Anytime you try to face your battles alone, you will only get what your strength can provide. They had gone from total dependence on God for the Jericho battle to not even asking God for His will at Ai.

The late Wesley Duewel was an author and long-time missionary to India. He wrote a great book entitled "Mighty Prevailing Prayer," which warns us against the sin of prayerlessness and stresses our need for prevailing prayer:

Prayerlessness means unavailability to God.

There is no easier sin to commit than the sin of prayerlessness. It is a sin against God and Man.

We have been so busy depending on our own natural strengths, our good training, and our busyness for God that we are near spiritual bankruptcy.

The more you intercede, the more intimate will be your walk with Christ and the stronger you will become by the Spirit's power.

Prayer is the master strategy that God gives for the defeat and rout of Satan.

Prevailing prayer is prayer that pushes right through all difficulties and obstacles, drives back all the opposing forces of Satan, and secures the will of God. Prevailing prayer is prayer that not only takes the initiative but continues on the offensive for God until spiritual victory is won.[2]

The second step towards defeat for the nation of Israel was overconfidence. The spies report back to Joshua that they only need a small army to defeat Ai. They forgot that God fought the battle of Jericho. Their victory at Jericho led to overconfidence in their next battle. Alan Carr explains it as follows:

Israel was still basking in the glow of their victory at Jericho, and they looked at Ai and felt like that little town would be no problem for such a great army. Israel was a confident people, but a closer look reveals that their confidence was misplaced. In verse 3, they feel that just a few of the soldiers are needed to secure a victory in little Ai.

Israel did not realize it, but they were living through one of the most dangerous times of life. You see, the time just after a great spiritual victory is a dangerous time. Often, like Israel, we will be overconfident and believe that we can handle any battle that comes our way. That belief system usually leads to our greatest defeats.[3]

Pride can drive us to heed earthly wisdom at times when we stand to benefit most from asking God to speak into our situations. From the outside, Ai looked like an easy victory. But Israel apparently did not pray to God for vision, clarity, or help before attacking Ai, and suffered heavy losses in following the advice of the spies. Anytime we combine prayerlessness and pride, we may be just one step away from defeat.

Questions:

1. Is your life filled with a prayerful dependence upon God for each step you take? Why or why not?

2. How does pride creep into your journey with Jesus?

3. How can you focus continually on your need for His presence?

Day Forty-One

Joshua

Dealing with Doubt

One of the consequences of sin is that it makes the sinner pity
himself instead of causing him to turn to God.
One of the signs of new life is that the individual
takes sides with God against himself.
Donald Grey Barnhouse[1]

Text: Joshua 7:6-7
⁶ Then Joshua tore his clothes and fell to the earth on his
face before the ark of the Lord until the evening, he and the elders of Israel. And they put dust on their heads. ⁷ And Joshua
said, "Alas, O Lord God, why have you brought this people over
the Jordan at all, to give us into the hands of the Amorites, to
destroy us? Would that we had been content to dwell beyond
the Jordan!"

Thoughts:
After the defeat at Ai, Joshua and the elders fell on their faces
before the ark of the Lord. If only they would have fallen on their
faces before God before the battle started. While neither Joshua
nor Israel's leaders were spiritually prepared for the battle, they
responded correctly after defeat. There is never a bad time to
fall facedown before the Lord.

When defeat happened, doubt crept into Joshua's mind.
Joshua 7:7 shares the skepticism in his heart. He questioned
why God even allowed Israel to cross the Jordan. Joshua even
suggested that they should have just settled before they crossed

into the Promised Land. Not only did he completely forget the unbelievable victory at Jericho, but he also wanted to disregard the crossing of the Jordan!

This thought process was handed down to Joshua from past generations. Joshua did not come across this line of thinking on his own. Let's go back to two different encounters earlier in Israel's wilderness journey and see this common theme of wanting to settle for less than God's best.

The first time Israel wanted to return to Egypt was before they even crossed the Red Sea. When the people saw that they were trapped between Pharoah's army and the Red Sea, look at their response recorded in Exodus 14:10-12:

> [10] When Pharaoh drew near, the people of Israel lifted up their eyes, and behold, the Egyptians were marching after them, and they feared greatly. And the people of Israel cried out to the Lord. [11] They said to Moses, "Is it because there are no graves in Egypt that you have taken us away to die in the wilderness? What have you done to us in bringing us out of Egypt? [12] Is not this what we said to you in Egypt: 'Leave us alone that we may serve the Egyptians'? For it would have been better for us to serve the Egyptians than to die in the wilderness."

The second time Israel wanted to return to Egypt is recorded in the book of Numbers. Numbers 13 tells the story of the 12 spies who were sent into Canaan. As you recall, Joshua was one of them. Israel listened to the majority report that said the giants in the land were too large to defeat. The people completely ignored Joshua and Caleb when they said, "We can take the land because God is on our side." Read the first four verses of Numbers 14 and you will see how Israel responded to their fears.

¹ Then all the congregation raised a loud cry, and the people wept that night. ² And all the people of Israel grumbled against Moses and Aaron. The whole congregation said to them, "Would that we had died in the land of Egypt! Or would that we had died in this wilderness! ³ Why is the Lord bringing us into this land, to fall by the sword? Our wives and our little ones will become a prey. Would it not be better for us to go back to Egypt?" ⁴ And they said to one another, "Let us choose a leader and go back to Egypt."

When they heard about the size of their enemies, Israel wanted to go back to Egypt. In our walk with Jesus, it is easy sometimes to settle for less than God's best and choose our safety over the future victories God has in store for us.

Here is a lesson we need to learn in our seasons of doubt: We can always be honest before the Lord. God can handle our doubts and our fears. Rather than lie to God and say what we think He wants to hear, sincere prayer leads to a genuine relationship with God. And God honors that honesty by speaking truths back into our lives. The Psalms are full of honest confessions of doubt before the Lord that resulted in pure praise. For example, notice just a few verses from Psalm 142:

²I pour out my complaint before Him; I tell my trouble before Him. . . ⁴Look to the right and see: there is none who takes notice of me; no refuge remains to me; no one cares for my soul. ⁵I cry to you, O Lord; I say, "You are my refuge, my portion in the land of the living."

When we speak to God with complete honesty, He has a unique way of changing our perspective and turning our doubts into praise.

Questions:

1. How do circumstances in your life sometimes cause you to doubt God's plan?

2. How can you be brutally honest about how you feel in your prayer life with God while also trusting Him enough to praise Him through your doubts?

3. Look at the advice Moses gave Israel when they wanted to return to Egypt before they crossed the Red Sea.

Exodus 14:13-14 (ESV)
    [13] And Moses said to the people, "Fear not, stand firm, and see the salvation of the Lord, which he will work for you today. For the Egyptians whom you see today, you shall never see again. [14] The Lord will fight for you, and you have only to be silent."

What lessons from Moses' response can you apply to Joshua's situation in Joshua 7:6-7?

Joshua

For His Great Name!

For Your name's sake, O Lord,
pardon my guilt, for it is great.
Psalm 25:11

For You are my rock and my fortress;
and for Your name's sake You lead me and guide me;
Psalm 31:3

Not to us, O Lord, not to us, but to Your name give glory,
for the sake of Your steadfast love and Your faithfulness!
Psalm 115:1

Text: Joshua 7:8-9
⁸ O Lord, what can I say, when Israel has turned their backs before their enemies! ⁹ For the Canaanites and all the inhabitants of the land will hear of it and will surround us and cut off our name from the earth. And what will you do for your great name?"

Thoughts:
Joshua goes from doubting God's plan to fearing that this one defeat will lead to Israel's demise. In Joshua 7:9, Joshua said that Israel's enemies would "cut off their name from the earth." In other words, Joshua thought no one would remember them after they were gone. Because of this one defeat, Joshua felt like everything God had done through his life and for His people would be for nothing.

Have you ever felt that way? Have you ever gone from a great victory to such a demoralizing defeat that it made you question everything about God and His plans for your life?

Joshua 7:7 ends with this direct question from a bewildered Joshua: "And what will you do for your great name?" Joshua sees that what he thought God was doing isn't lining up with what God is actually doing, and he is baffled. But he understands that God is abundantly capable of vindicating His own name. So he asks, "Well, what do YOU want to do, God?"

The Psalms speak often about what God does for His namesake! God does all that He does for the sake of His name. Notice the following Scripture:

Psalm 23:3 (ESV)

He restores my soul. He leads me in paths of righteousness for His name's sake.

Psalm 79:9 (ESV)

Help us, O God of our salvation, for the glory of Your name; deliver us, and atone for our sins, for Your name's sake!

Psalm 109:21 (ESV)

But You, O God my Lord, deal on my behalf for Your name's sake; because Your steadfast love is good, deliver me!

Psalm 143:11 (ESV)

For Your name's sake, O Lord, preserve my life! In Your righteousness bring my soul out of trouble!

When God acts for the sake of His name, He is acting in His character that can never change. God always honors His own name because there is no greater name than His. His works point back to His matchless name. God will always protect the glory of His name. Notice what Isaiah 48:9-11 reveals about God's approach to His name:

> [9]"For My name's sake I defer my anger;
> for the sake of My praise I restrain it for you,
> that I may not cut you off.
> [10] Behold, I have refined you, but not as silver;
> I have tried you in the furnace of affliction.
> [11] For My own sake, for My own sake, I do it,
> for how should My name be profaned?
> My glory I will not give to another."

One thing we should never question is whether God can and will defend His name!

Questions:

1. How does God's approach to His name emphasize that this life is not about you; rather it is all about Him?

2. How does Philippians 2:9-11 give you confidence that God's name is never in jeopardy?

> [9] Therefore God has highly exalted him and bestowed on him the name that is above every name, [10] so that at the name of Jesus every knee should bow, in heaven and on earth and under the earth, [11] and every tongue confess that Jesus Christ is Lord, to the glory of God the Father.

Day Forty-Three

Joshua

Learning Responsibility

Today's church wants to be raptured from responsibility.
Leonard Ravenhill[1]

Text: Joshua 7:10-15

[10] The Lord said to Joshua, "Get up! Why have you fallen on your face? [11] Israel has sinned; they have transgressed my covenant that I commanded them; they have taken some of the devoted things; they have stolen and lied and put them among their own belongings. [12] Therefore the people of Israel cannot stand before their enemies. They turn their backs before their enemies, because they have become devoted for destruction. I will be with you no more, unless you destroy the devoted things from among you. [13] Get up! Consecrate the people and say, 'Consecrate yourselves for tomorrow; for thus says the Lord, God of Israel, "There are devoted things in your midst, O Israel. You cannot stand before your enemies until you take away the devoted things from among you."

[14] In the morning therefore you shall be brought near by your tribes. And the tribe that the Lord takes by lot shall come near by clans. And the clan that the Lord takes shall come near by households. And the household that the Lord takes shall come near man by man. [15] And he who is taken with the devoted things shall be burned with fire, he and all that he has, because he has transgressed the covenant of the Lord, and because he has done an outrageous thing in Israel.'"

Thoughts:

There is a serious lesson that everyone can learn from today's Scripture. One man, Achan, had stolen property and had taken spoils of victory. These stolen items were devoted things that were supposed to be set apart for the Lord. One person disobeyed God. Yet, the verdict from Heaven was not, "Achan has sinned." The ruling from Heaven was, "Israel has sinned." One man fell short of the glory of God, and an entire army was defeated. What lesson does this provide?

God saw Israel as one family and one nation. He was their Father, and they all were His children. They were redeemed as one people, the weakest among them along with the strongest among them. Thus, God dealt with them as a corporate body. So at Ai, the judgment pronounced from Heaven was to the entire community: "Israel has sinned."

This is a great lesson that God's corporate Church needs to learn. When one member of a fellowship of faith sins before God, the verdict from Heaven is, "My people have sinned." When one follower of Jesus Christ commits a sin against God, it affects the witness of the entire community. As His people, we are in this together. As one team for one Lord, we are victorious together and we also suffer defeat together.

David Firth explains this concept of corporate responsibility as follows:

> Just as Rahab's confession was sufficient for her whole family to be delivered, so also Achan's sin is sufficient to affect the whole nation. Sin is not an isolated act, something done in private without effect on others. Instead, the individual's sinful decision impacts the whole community. That is why we are told Israel had been unfaithful with the devoted things before our focus is directed to Achan.[2]

What does the text teach us about the sin that impacted the entire nation of Israel? In his commentary on Joshua, Colin Peckham explains the meanings of several terms from Joshua 7. As you read each one, may they give you insight into this sin that led to Israel's defeat.

God says that Israel sinned, transgressed, and disobeyed; and also, that they stole, deceived, and concealed.

Sin means to miss the mark. It was seen to be deliberate, with the idea of personal responsibility.

Transgression here means to pass over or to pass by. God had commanded that they take nothing from Jericho, and they simply passed by the command.

Disobedience. They deliberately disobeyed God's instructions.

Stealing. God had said, 'All the silver and gold … shall come into the treasury of the LORD' (6:19). Achan stole from God. Malachi says plainly, 'You have robbed me!' (Malachi 3:8). He took that which was consecrated to God. Many are sinning against Him by withholding that which is rightfully His.

Deceiving. Achan deceived the people until forced to admit his crime.

Concealment. Achan thought that no one at all would ever know!

Trespass (v. 1). The Hebrew word here means 'treachery'. Achan was a traitor—unfaithful to his commander and to his Lord. Some are unfaithful in their ministry and in their walk with God—it's treachery!

Folly or *disgrace.* Achan thought that he was clever. No one knew! But sin is foolish and brings disgrace.[4]

Questions:

1. What are your thoughts on individual sins affecting the entire nation? How does today's devotion heighten your awareness of your personal responsibility?

2. How does the discussion of terms for Joshua 7 add to your insight of this Scripture? What lessons did you learn and how can you apply these in your spiritual life?

Day Forty-Four

Joshua

God Knows Everything

God knows what you've been doing, everything you've been doing. You may fool me, but you can't fool God!
F. Scott Fitzgerald[1]

God knows everything. So why not run to Him and tell Him all the things that He already knows?
Kevin DeYoung[2]

Text: Joshua 7:16-21

[16] So Joshua rose early in the morning and brought Israel near tribe by tribe, and the tribe of Judah was taken. [17] And he brought near the clans of Judah, and the clan of the Zerahites was taken. And he brought near the clan of the Zerahites man by man, and Zabdi was taken. [18] And he brought near his household man by man, and Achan the son of Carmi, son of Zabdi, son of Zerah, of the tribe of Judah, was taken. [19] Then Joshua said to Achan, "My son, give glory to the Lord God of Israel and give praise to him. And tell me now what you have done; do not hide it from me." [20] And Achan answered Joshua, "Truly I have sinned against the Lord God of Israel, and this is what I did: [21] when I saw among the spoil a beautiful cloak from Shinar, and 200 shekels of silver, and a bar of gold weighing 50 shekels, then I coveted them and took them. And see, they are hidden in the earth inside my tent, with the silver underneath."

Thoughts:

Joshua was led by God to pick out one person from a nation of over two million people. You have heard the phrase, "Finding a needle in a haystack." This would be like finding part of a needle in several haystacks. Yet God divinely singled out the one sinner among the millions of people in a very systematic way.

We can only make an educated guess concerning what method was used to determine who it was. The most likely possibility was that Joshua used the urim and thummim. The urim and thummim were two stones used in the breastplate of the priests. Urim was a white stone and thummim was a black stone. In Hebrew, their names mean "lights" and "perfections." They are first mentioned in Exodus 28:30.

> [30] And in the breastpiece of judgment you shall put the Urim and the Thummim, and they shall be on Aaron's heart, when he goes in before the Lord. Thus Aaron shall bear the judgment of the people of Israel on his heart before the Lord regularly.

These two stones were used by the high priests to answer questions or to reveal God's divine will. Like sanctified dice, you would throw these stones to discover God's answer to certain questions. The Lord directed this process and divinely worked through the process to disclose His will.

Imagine with me what it must have been like for Achan when Joshua 7:16-21 was taking place. Achan knows he is the sinner everyone is looking for. The stones are thrown, and the tribe of Judah is chosen. Achan says to himself, "Wow, that's my tribe," and the whole tribe steps forward. The stones are tossed again, and the clan of Zerahites are chosen. And the field is being narrowed down considerably. Next, Zabdi is chosen. That's Achan's father. Now they are down to just Achan's father and siblings. Finally, Achan himself is chosen. I imagine that the knots in Achan's stomach were tightening with each step in the process.

One sinner in a few million people. God knows everything. Be sure, your sin will be found out. Jesus made this statement recorded in Luke 12:2: "Nothing is covered up that will not be revealed, or hidden that will not be known."

Achan was now the only man standing in front of the entire nation of Israel. And Joshua said, "Tell me now what you have done; do not hide it from me." And Achan finally confessed. It is good that Achan confessed, but it was a day late and a dollar short. It was not genuine repentance. It's not real remorse. Achan was busted and called out before everyone. Of course, he confessed.

Notice carefully Achan's confession found in Joshua 7:21:

> . . . when I saw among the spoil a beautiful cloak from Shinar, and 200 shekels of silver, and a bar of gold weighing 50 shekels, then I coveted them and took them.

Achan "saw," "coveted," and "took." This describes the original sin by Adam and Eve recorded in Genesis 3:6:

> [6] So when the woman saw that the tree was good for food, and that it was a delight to the eyes, and that the tree was to be desired to make one wise, she took of its fruit and ate, and she also gave some to her husband who was with her, and he ate.

And just like Adam and Eve, he tried to hide his sin from God. Achan confessed his sin too late and was forced to uncover his transgression. The example of Achan shows us the danger of harboring unconfessed, unrepentant sin. If he had come forward and confessed of his own accord, the consequences may not have been as severe.

Questions:

1. How many chances did Achan have to confess before he was marked as a sinner?

2. What are your thoughts on the process God used to point Achan out to Joshua?

3. How does Achan's answer in Joshua 7:21 explain how you give in to temptation in your personal life? What steps do you need to take to guard your eyes, heart, and hands spiritually?

4. Will you uncover your sin before God does? How does 1 John 1:9-10 impact your answer?

> ⁹ If we confess our sins, He is faithful and just to forgive us our sins and to cleanse us from all unrighteousness. ¹⁰ If we say we have not sinned, we make Him a liar, and His word is not in us.

Day Forty-Five

Joshua

The High Cost of Coveting

Desire of having is the sin of covetousness.
William Shakespeare[1]

. . . covetousness is never to be satisfied; the more it has,
the more it wants. Such insatiable ones injure themselves,
and transform God's blessings into evil.
Martin Luther[2]

Text: Joshua 7:22-26
[22] So Joshua sent messengers, and they ran to the tent; and behold, it was hidden in his tent with the silver underneath.
[23] And they took them out of the tent and brought them to Joshua and to all the people of Israel. And they laid them down before the Lord. [24] And Joshua and all Israel with him took Achan the son of Zerah, and the silver and the cloak and the bar of gold, and his sons and daughters and his oxen and donkeys and sheep and his tent and all that he had. And they brought them up to the Valley of Achor. [25] And Joshua said, "Why did you bring trouble on us? The Lord brings trouble on you today." And all Israel stoned him with stones. They burned them with fire and stoned them with stones. [26] And they raised over him a great heap of stones that remains to this day. Then the Lord turned from his burning anger. Therefore, to this day the name of that place is called the Valley of Achor.

Thoughts:

Coveting can be a fatal sin if not kept in check. God warns against coveting at least sixteen different times in Scripture. Notice how dangerous and useless coveting can be:

First Achan said, *"I saw."* He must have been mesmerized. Second, he said, *"I coveted."* There is no question as to whether or not he really needed the garment, the silver, and the gold. He couldn't use it. James said that "every good and perfect gift comes from above." What good is a treasure that you cannot use, and that you must keep hidden?

It's no accident that the final and most inward of all the Ten Commandments deals with covetousness. Part of the Old Testament law reads, "You shall burn the carved images of their gods with fire; you shall not covet the silver or gold that is on them, nor take it for yourselves, lest you be snared by it; for it is an abomination to the LORD your God" (Deut. 7:25). Jesus restated this in more contemporary words: "Take heed and beware of covetousness, for one's life does not consist in the abundance of the things he possesses" (Luke 12:15). Covetousness destroys joy in the Christian. The grass is always greener on the other side of the fence. When we spend our time looking across the fence at what we don't own, we miss seeing how gracious God has been in what is legitimately ours.

Achan said, "I saw, I coveted, I took, and I hid." Silver and gold are not bad in themselves, but how often they take over our minds and lead us away from God into an idolatry of things. Achan's story is ours wherein we are unwilling to say with the apostle Paul, "I have learned in whatever state I am, to be content" (Philippians 4:11).[3]

Colin Peckham, in his devotional commentary on Joshua, describes the attractiveness of sin that lured Achan:

> Achan saw a 'beautiful Babylonian garment', and he lusted after this and the silver and gold. Sin attracts and allures; it fascinates and fools; it draws and condemns. We must have it. It becomes an obsession.
>
> So it was with Achan. He could withstand it no longer. He saw and he coveted. The consequences of being disobedient faded into the background. That which was before him, he had to have. It became a force which he could not control. 'He who is greedy for gain troubles his own house' (Proverbs 15:27), and that day Achan brought great trouble to his house. He was greedy for gain and disobeyed God in order to get it. All kinds of devices are invented, all kinds of twisted plans are devised to grasp the things the heart desires. 'But those who desire to be rich fall into temptation and a snare, and into many foolish and harmful lusts which drown men in destruction and perdition' (1 Timothy 6:9).[4]

The foundation of Achan's demise was a covetous heart. If he had been content with following God into the Promised Land, he would have been blessed beyond measure. Instead, his coveting heart led to the defeat of his nation, the loss of his family, and ultimately his own life.

We discover in Joshua 7:26 that Achan's judgment and death abated the Lord's anger against all Israel. This remind us that Jesus took our judgment by dying in our place. We rebelled against God's commands, just as Achan did. God's Word is clear that we deserved the penalty of sin, which is death. But thanks be to God, Jesus died in our place.

Questions:

1. In what ways are you prone to coveting?

2. How can gratitude and contentment build a spiritual barrier against a covetous spirit?

3. How does 1 Corinthians 6:9-11 impact your view of coveting? (Note the Greek word for "greedy" in verse 10 is a word that means "to covet.")

> ⁹ Or do you not know that the unrighteous will not inherit the kingdom of God? Do not be deceived: neither the sexually immoral, nor idolaters, nor adulterers, nor men who practice homosexuality, ¹⁰ nor thieves, nor the greedy, nor drunkards, nor revilers, nor swindlers will inherit the kingdom of God.

> ¹¹ And such were some of you. But you were washed, you were sanctified, you were justified in the name of the Lord Jesus Christ and by the Spirit of our God.

Day Forty-Six

Joshua

God Can Turn Your Trouble to Hope

The name *Achor* means "trouble." The Valley of Achor is mentioned in Isaiah 65:10 and Hosea 2:15 as a place where the Jews will one day have a new beginning and no longer be associated with shame and defeat. The Valley of Achor will become for them "a door of hope" when they return to their land and share in the blessings of the messianic kingdom.
Warren Wiersbe[1]

Text: Joshua 8:1-2
[1] And the Lord said to Joshua, "Do not fear and do not be dismayed. Take all the fighting men with you, and arise, go up to Ai. See, I have given into your hand the king of Ai, and his people, his city, and his land. [2] And you shall do to Ai and its king as you did to Jericho and its king. Only its spoil and its livestock you shall take as plunder for yourselves. Lay an ambush against the city, behind it."

Thoughts:
Joshua 7:24 tells us that Achan and his family were executed at the Valley of Achor. The Valley of Achor, in Hebrew, means "the valley of trouble." This coincides with what Joshua asked and stated in Joshua 7:25: "Why did you bring trouble on us? The Lord brings trouble on you today." Remember that name "Achor" and follow God's plan of redemption! In the Old Testament book of Hosea, it shows up again. Hosea depicts Israel as an adulterous bride who has betrayed God. Then Hosea depicts God's gracious restoring love:

Hosea 2:15 (ESV)

And there I will give her her vineyards and make the Valley of Achor a door of hope. And there she shall answer as in the days of her youth, as at the time when she came out of the land of Egypt.

God will make the Valley of Achor a door of hope! What does that mean? In a place where the full weight of Achan's sin came down, resulting in judgment and death for him and his family, God promises to place a door of hope. At the place where sin is uncovered, judged, and purged from Israel, there is always hope. This was as true for the Israelites in Hosea's time as it was for the Israelites when Joshua was leading them.

"Israel initially suffered defeat at Ai because of Achan's sin. But that was not the end of Israel's story at Ai." After the sin was judged by God, He wrote a new chapter in the story of Israel. I am overjoyed that Joshua 8 comes after Joshua 7. After we cause hurt, God brings hope! After man's sin shuts one door, God's forgiveness opens another one. After repentance comes restoration!

As soon as the sin is dealt with, God's anger is removed. God takes the initiative in coming to Joshua with words of great encouragement and fresh direction. (See Joshua 8:1-2.) What God is teaching us about Himself in these opening verses is what David was later to affirm in Psalm 23:3:

He restores my soul. He leads me in paths of righteousness for His name's sake.

God is a great restorer, and He restores us with great sensitivity and relevance. You will discover this throughout Joshua chapter 8: in the exhortation of verse 1, the affirmations of verse 2, and the battle plans of verses 8 and 18.

God's restoration deals first with the inward need of the soul, which is then translated into the outward circumstances of life. Now that the Israelites have been consecrated to God again (Joshua 7:13) and the sin has been purged from their midst, God will certainly fulfill His covenant promises to them. Therefore, God encourages Joshua to press on with the conquest, assuring him of victory.

The way to strengthen broken hearts is to go forward in faith, not lamenting the past or wishing that things were different, but rather building on the promises of God and putting our maximum effort into obeying His commands. As someone once said, "Our responsibility is our response to His ability." This response requires both faith and obedience. The two are essentially linked together.

Questions:

1. What are your thoughts about God changing the Valley of Trouble into a Door of Hope?

2. In what ways has God restored your soul?

3. How does Psalm 33:18-22 add to today's devotion?

¹⁸ Behold, the eye of the Lord is on those who fear Him, on those who hope in His steadfast love, ¹⁹ that He may deliver their soul from death and keep them alive in famine. ²⁰ Our soul waits for the Lord; He is our help and our shield. ²¹ For our heart is glad in Him, because we trust in His holy name. ²² Let Your steadfast love, O Lord, be upon us, even as we hope in You.

Day Forty-Seven

Joshua

Renewed Hope

Wisdom is the capacity to see things from God's viewpoint.
Charles Stanley[1]

Text: Joshua 8:3-9
³ So Joshua and all the fighting men arose to go up to Ai. And Joshua chose 30,000 mighty men of valor and sent them out by night. ⁴ And he commanded them, "Behold, you shall lie in ambush against the city, behind it. Do not go very far from the city, but all of you remain ready. ⁵ And I and all the people who are with me will approach the city. And when they come out against us just as before, we shall flee before them. ⁶ And they will come out after us, until we have drawn them away from the city. For they will say, 'They are fleeing from us, just as before.' So we will flee before them. ⁷ Then you shall rise up from the ambush and seize the city, for the Lord your God will give it into your hand. ⁸ And as soon as you have taken the city, you shall set the city on fire. You shall do according to the word of the Lord. See, I have commanded you." ⁹ So Joshua sent them out. And they went to the place of ambush and lay between Bethel and Ai, to the west of Ai, but Joshua spent that night among the people.

Thoughts:
Joshua had a new plan and a renewed passion to battle against Ai a second time. In Hebrew, Ai means "the ruin." This city had brought loss to Israel, but now Joshua and Israel were restored. God's restoration of Israel would lead to Ai's ruin.

Israel's renewed hope would require obedient faith. They were prayerless and disobedient before, and that combination led to defeat. Now, they would need to trust God completely and obey Him fully to be victorious. Bible scholar David Guzik makes the following statement about Israel's need to fully surrender to God's plan:

> This time Joshua did not send 3,000 men as before (Joshua 7:4). Now he sent 30,000 "mighty men of valor." When we need to regain victory, we must use every resource, and the best resources for victory.[2]

God gave Joshua a new plan after He had given him a renewed promise. Colin Peckham's great commentary brings awareness to both the strategy and the promise:

> **There was a word of strategy.**
> 'Lay an ambush.' The strategy was humbling. They had to hide away behind Ai instead of triumphantly marching around the city as they had done at Jericho. God does not always work in the same way. Having won one victory, we cannot presume to use the same methods in the next battle. On this occasion, Joshua would come against the city and make as though he was fleeing before the men of Ai, who would come out against them as before. When they had left the city the men in ambush would then rise and take the city, surrounding the men of Ai. This was God's plan, and they obeyed it to the letter.
> Even though they had the promise of God that He would give them the city and its land, they had to actively be engaged in the conflict. God's promises are not given for us to conclude that the results are secure and that we

have nothing more to do. Faith is no substitute for hard work. Hope does not absolve us of our obligations but inspires us to perform better. Our 'labor is not in vain in the Lord' (1 Corinthians 15:58). 'Take up the whole armor of God … and … stand' (Ephesians 6:13).

There was a word of promise.
'See, I have given into your hand the king of Ai, his people, his city, and his land' (Joshua 8:1).

How blessed is that word from God; how wonderfully assuring; what certainty it brings. Why, when He has spoken, you can go through fire and water. You can endure all indignities, all rejections, all hardships. You can go to the uttermost part of the earth, for He is with you. He has spoken, and that puts steel into your soul. He is strengthening you to accomplish all that He has whispered to you. His word to you is the enablement for His plan for you.[3]

Questions:

1. Describe a time in your life when God gave you renewed hope.

2. What does it say about God's character that He restores people after their failures?

3. Why do you think God changed His strategy between Jericho and Ai?

4. List specific promises from His word that give you renewed hope.

Day Forty-Eight

Joshua

Learning from Defeat

If there be, therefore, perpetual failure in your life,
it cannot arise from any weakness or impotence in the
Mighty God; but from some failure on your part. That failure
may probably be discovered in one of three hiding places -
imperfect surrender, deficient faith, or neglected communion.
But when the intention of the soul is right with God,
without doubt He will save.
F.B. Meyer[1]

Text: Joshua 8:10-17
10 Joshua arose early in the morning and mustered the people and went up, he and the elders of Israel, before the people to Ai. **11** And all the fighting men who were with him went up and drew near before the city and encamped on the north side of Ai, with a ravine between them and Ai. **12** He took about 5,000 men and set them in ambush between Bethel and Ai, to the west of the city. **13** So they stationed the forces, the main encampment that was north of the city and its rear guard west of the city. But Joshua spent that night in the valley. **14** And as soon as the king of Ai saw this, he and all his people, the men of the city, hurried and went out early to the appointed place toward the Arabah to meet Israel in battle. But he did not know that there was an ambush against him behind the city. **15** And Joshua and all Israel pretended to be beaten before them and fled in the direction of the wilderness. **16** So all the people who were in the city were

called together to pursue them, and as they pursued Joshua they were drawn away from the city. **17** Not a man was left in Ai or Bethel who did not go out after Israel. They left the city open and pursued Israel.

Thoughts:

Some of our greatest life lessons come from our failures. However, this can only happen if we are willing to learn from our mistakes. If not, we will be defeated and probably repeat our old patterns.

In Joshua 8:10-17, Israel learned more from defeat than Ai did from success. The first time Joshua battled Ai, Israel was overconfident and only brought 3,000 men. This time, Joshua depended on God's plan and brought ten times as many soldiers. You will discover in Joshua 8:25 that Ai had 12,000 people. So, in the first battle, Israel battled against great odds only having one Israelite for every four citizens of Ai. Israel learned their lesson from their defeat and now had 2.5 soldiers for every resident of Ai.

On the other hand, Ai became cocky after they defeated Israel in the first battle. When Ai saw that Israel had come to fight again, they took every man out of their city to fight. They did not realize that Israel had brought more people than last time and had an ambush set up behind them. Ai thought they would easily defeat Israel this time just like they had done previously. They were sadly mistaken and suffered the loss of their entire city.

It is often easier to learn lessons after failure than victory. That is why we are the most vulnerable to the devil's attacks after we have been victorious.

Ellen Bargh, a Christian author from the UK, wrote the following about lessons from failure:

The Bible never promised us that we would be successful in everything we do. Instead, it tells us how we ought to deal with failure when it happens.

Proverbs 24:16 says a righteous man falls seven times but still gets up. Paul tells us in Philippians 3 to forget what has happened before and to strive towards the goal of Jesus Christ.

Failing is not the problem. The problem is when we *fail to learn from our failures and* give up altogether.[2]

Bargh went on to give "Four Lessons Only Failures Can Teach." These four lessons were:

Learn to ask for help.
Learn that you need God's grace.
Learn that you can still be redeemed.
Learn to persevere.

Ellen Bargh closed her discussion with these words of wisdom:

Even though I fail and will continue to fail, I take comfort and courage in the fact that God is bigger, and He can redeem me and my failures. He paid the price so that I can pick myself up and keep following Him.[3]

Questions:

1. What lessons do you think Israel and Joshua learned after their first defeat at Ai? How did they apply these lessons so that they were in a position for God to bring victory during the second battle?

2. Why is it essential that we are constantly learning in our walk with the Lord?

3. Ellen Bargh provided four lessons that we can learn from failures. Which of her four lessons do you still need to learn? Why do you think the lesson or lessons you picked are difficult for you to apply to your life?

Day Forty-Nine

Joshua

God's Power through an Outstretched Arm

[17] If you say in your heart, 'These nations are greater than I. How can I dispossess them?' [18] you shall not be afraid of them but you shall remember what the Lord your God did to Pharaoh and to all Egypt, [19] the great trials that your eyes saw, the signs, the wonders, the mighty hand, and the outstretched arm, by which the Lord your God brought you out. So will the Lord your God do to all the peoples of whom you are afraid.
Deuteronomy 7:17-19

Text: Joshua 8:18-29
[18] Then the Lord said to Joshua, "Stretch out the javelin that is in your hand toward Ai, for I will give it into your hand." And Joshua stretched out the javelin that was in his hand toward the city. [19] And the men in the ambush rose quickly out of their place, and as soon as he had stretched out his hand, they ran and entered the city and captured it. And they hurried to set the city on fire. [20] So when the men of Ai looked back, behold, the smoke of the city went up to heaven, and they had no power to flee this way or that, for the people who fled to the wilderness turned back against the pursuers.

[21] And when Joshua and all Israel saw that the ambush had captured the city, and that the smoke of the city went up, then they turned back and struck down the men of Ai. [22] And the others came out from the city against them, so they were in the midst of Israel, some on this side, and some on that side. And

Israel struck them down, until there was left none that survived or escaped. ²³ But the king of Ai they took alive, and brought him near to Joshua.

²⁴ When Israel had finished killing all the inhabitants of Ai in the open wilderness where they pursued them, and all of them to the very last had fallen by the edge of the sword, all Israel returned to Ai and struck it down with the edge of the sword. ²⁵ And all who fell that day, both men and women, were 12,000, all the people of Ai. ²⁶ But Joshua did not draw back his hand with which he stretched out the javelin until he had devoted all the inhabitants of Ai to destruction. ²⁷ Only the livestock and the spoil of that city Israel took as their plunder, according to the word of the Lord that he commanded Joshua. ²⁸ So Joshua burned Ai and made it forever a heap of ruins, as it is to this day. ²⁹ And he hanged the king of Ai on a tree until evening. And at sunset Joshua commanded, and they took his body down from the tree and threw it at the entrance of the gate of the city and raised over it a great heap of stones, which stands there to this day.

Thoughts:

God divinely brought about a dramatic victory for Israel against Ai. Joshua held out his hand with his javelin pointing towards the city until every inhabitant of Ai was destroyed. (See verses 18 and 26.) There was no possible way for Joshua, in his own strength, to hold a javelin with an outstretched arm the time it would take for the entire battle of Ai to take place.

Compare this with Israel's battle against Amalek in Exodus 17:

¹⁰ So Joshua did as Moses told him, and fought with Amalek, while Moses, Aaron, and Hur went up to the top of the hill. ¹¹ Whenever Moses held up his hand, Israel prevailed, and whenever he lowered his hand, Amalek

prevailed. [12] But Moses' hands grew weary, so they took a stone and put it under him, and he sat on it, while Aaron and Hur held up his hands, one on one side, and the other on the other side. So his hands were steady until the going down of the sun. [13] And Joshua overwhelmed Amalek and his people with the sword.

Moses needed the help of Aaron and Hur to keep his hands raised for the battle with Amalek. During Israel's fight against Ai, God gave Joshua the strength and endurance to keep his javelin arm raised. It was only by the hand of God that Joshua held out his hand. This feat showed the power of God's hand to save and His arm to provide.

Scripture is full of references to God's mighty outstretched arm. Note the two examples below:

Psalm 136:12 (ESV)
. . . with a strong hand and an outstretched arm, for His steadfast love endures forever . . .

Isaiah 14:26-27 (ESV)
This is the purpose that is purposed concerning the whole earth, and this is the hand that is stretched out over all the nations. For the Lord of Hosts has purposed, and who will annul it? His hand is stretched out, and who will turn it back?

As Scripture declares, God's hand is over every nation on the earth. By His own hand, He brought judgment against Ai, and He gave victory to Israel.

David Howard, in the New American Commentary series, shares an insightful word from Joshua 8:18-19:

Joshua was to hold out the weapon in his hand as a signal for the ambush force to begin their attack on Ai. God's provision was evident here, as we can see in a play on the words "your hand": Joshua was to stretch out the weapon "in your hand" *(běyadka)* because God was going to give the city "into your hand" *(běyadkā)*. The weapon itself was not going to win the victory; God was going to give it.[1]

May we learn along with Joshua and all of Israel that unless God's hand is upon us, we will not prevail.

Questions:

1. In what ways has God extended His hand to you and provided for your victories?

2. What does Acts 4:29-30 say about God's mighty hand and outstretched arm?

[29] And now, Lord, look upon their threats and grant to your servants to continue to speak your word with all boldness, [30] while you stretch out your hand to heal, and signs and wonders are performed through the name of your holy servant Jesus.

Day Fifty

Joshua

Worship on Mount Ebal

God calls us first, not to a platform, but to an altar.
J. D. Greear[1]

*I need to worship because without it I can forget
that I have a big God beside me and live in fear.
I need to worship because without it I can forget
His calling and begin to live in a spirit of self-preoccupation.
I need to worship because without it I lose a sense of
wonder and gratitude and plod through life with blinders on.
I need worship because my natural tendency is
toward self-reliance and stubborn independence.*
John Ortberg[2]

Text: Joshua 8:30-31
[30] At that time Joshua built an altar to the Lord, the God of Israel, on Mount Ebal, [31] just as Moses the servant of the Lord had commanded the people of Israel, as it is written in the Book of the Law of Moses, "an altar of uncut stones, upon which no man has wielded an iron tool." And they offered on it burnt offerings to the Lord and sacrificed peace offerings.

Thoughts:
It is interesting that after the defeat of Ai, Israel took a break from physical battles to worship spiritually before God. Rather than keep their military momentum and forge ahead

207

into the Promised Land, they take a challenging journey for an extended time of marvelous worship.

God had given Israel specific instructions through Moses about Mount Ebal. In Deuteronomy 11:26-32, Moses commands the Israelites to be faithful and obedient to God for who He is and for all the mighty deeds He has done:

> 26 "See, I am setting before you today a blessing and a curse: 27 the blessing, if you obey the commandments of the Lord your God, which I command you today, 28 and the curse, if you do not obey the commandments of the Lord your God, but turn aside from the way that I am commanding you today, to go after other gods that you have not known.
>
> 29 And when the Lord your God brings you into the land that you are entering to take possession of it, you shall set the blessing on Mount Gerizim and the curse on Mount Ebal. 30 Are they not beyond the Jordan, west of the road, toward the going down of the sun, in the land of the Canaanites who live in the Arabah, opposite Gilgal, beside the oak of Moreh? 31 For you are to cross over the Jordan to go in to take possession of the land that the Lord your God is giving you. And when you possess it and live in it, 32 you shall be careful to do all the statutes and the rules that I am setting before you today.

God places a high priority on His people worshipping Him. God commanded Israel to go to this specific place to meet with Him. In the heat of battle, with enemies all around them, God wanted Israel to see the urgency and necessity of worship.

An altar was established on Mount Ebal. Mount Gerizim was the place for blessings, and one would expect to find the altar there. On the other hand, Mount Ebal was the place for curses.

Colin Peckham gives us a deep look into the spiritual implications of Joshua 8:30-31 in his commentary:

> The altar was for sinners under the curse. The altar was built, and the offering given on Mount Ebal, prefiguring the One who came to enter the place of the curse. Not only is Christ the Altar, but He is also the Sacrifice; He bore the curses of God for taking our sin upon Himself.
>
> The people offered burnt offerings and sacrificed peace offerings. The voluntary burnt offering was to be completely consumed on the altar. This signified total surrender. Jesus totally surrendered Himself as the sacrificial Lamb of God when He went to Calvary. He held nothing back but gave Himself completely as an offering for our redemption. And this is what we must do when we come to Him and give our all. It indicates complete consecration.
>
> The peace offering was not wholly consumed by the fire. A part was eaten by those who brought the offering, to signify that they had fellowship and communion with God. They fed on the sacrificial lamb. We too feed on the Lamb of God. They were given instructions concerning this offering: 'You shall offer peace offerings, and shall eat there, and rejoice before the LORD your God' (Deuteronomy 27:7). How amazing! They ate and rejoiced at the place of the curse! Jesus took the curse for us—was slain—yet in this terrible offering we rejoice, for it is for our salvation. We take the life of the sacrificial Lamb who died, but who lives, and through His life, we live! We feast on Him who is our life. Gratefully and humbly, we rejoice at the place called Calvary—the place of the curse—where our sins

are judged and removed and where we feast on the life of the risen Lord.

A thousand years later the Samaritans built their altar on Mount Gerizim, not Mount Ebal. The woman of Samaria pointed to Mount Gerizim when she said to Jesus, 'Our fathers worshipped on this mountain, and you Jews say that in Jerusalem is the place where one ought to worship' (John 4:20). Self-righteous Samaritans would not come as sinners to Mount Ebal, the place of the curse, but they built their altar on Mount Gerizim, with its hoped-for blessings. So, Jesus had to say to her, 'You worship what you do not know' (John 4:22). Today, the self-righteous among us will not come as sinners, confessing their guilt and sin, to the substitutionary sacrifice on Mount Calvary (the place of the curse), but they go as righteous people seeking blessing at the altar of their own making. They go, as it were, to Mount Gerizim, hoping for blessing, and they 'worship what they do not know.'[3]

Questions:

1. Do you struggle to remember to worship God when you get busy with everything that's going on in your life? Why or why not?

2. What does the timing of Israel's worship say about the significance of celebrating God?

3. In your opinion, what is the implication of God's command to worship on these two mountains? How did His command in Deuteronomy 11:26-32, impact Jesus' conversation in John 4 with the woman at the well?

4. In your time of praising God, do you have a personal Mount Gerizim? Do you have a spiritual Mount Ebal? Explain your responses.

Joshua

His Word and His Presence

The Bible is alive, it speaks to me; it has feet, it runs after me; it has hands, it lays hold of me.
Martin Luther[1]

Text: Joshua 8:32-33

[32] And there, in the presence of the people of Israel, he wrote on the stones a copy of the law of Moses, which he had written. [33] And all Israel, sojourner as well as native born, with their elders and officers and their judges, stood on opposite sides of the ark before the Levitical priests who carried the ark of the covenant of the Lord, half of them in front of Mount Gerizim and half of them in front of Mount Ebal, just as Moses the servant of the Lord had commanded at the first, to bless the people of Israel.

Thoughts:

Remember, this journey to Shechem was a command given by Moses back in Deuteronomy 27. So the invasion into the Promised Land was put on pause while the whole nation of Israel went on a twenty-mile hike from Gilgal to worship God. Once the approximately 3 million people reached the valley, Joshua built an altar. And on the stones of this altar, Joshua copied the law of Moses.

Max Lucado shares these notes:

In the ancient Near East, it was customary for kings to commemorate their military achievements by recording their conquests on huge stones covered with plaster. Joshua, however, didn't memorialize his work. He celebrated God's law. The secret to the successful campaign of the Hebrews was not the strength of the army but the resolve of the people to keep God's commandments.[2]

Then all of Israel split into two groups with half of them standing in front of Mount Gerizim and the other half in front of Mount Ebal. They have the mountains behind them and the ark of the covenant in front of them. Everybody in the entire nation is facing the symbol of the presence of God. While they are facing the ark, they are also focused on God's Word written on the altar. Brian Harbour describes the moment with these words:

Everything at this point was ideal. The people were together. Their attention was focused on God. The Law of God was understood. It was a mountaintop experience that reminded them again of who God was and who they were.[3]

Warren Wiersbe adds the following from his wealth of biblical wisdom:

Joshua now reaffirmed the Law in the land of promise. Since the area between Mt. Ebal and Mt. Gerizim was a natural amphitheater, everybody could hear the words of the Law clearly and respond with intelligence. By shouting "Amen" to the statements that were read, the people admitted that they understood the Law with its blessings and curses, and that they accepted the responsibility of obeying it. This included the women, children, and sojourners who had joined Israel. If they wanted to share in Israel's conquest, they had to submit to the Law of Israel's God.

God's people today spiritually stand in a valley between two mounts—Mount Calvary, where Jesus died for our sins, and the Mount of Olives, where He will return in power and great glory (Zechariah 14:4). The Old Testament prophets saw the Messiah's suffering and glory, but they did not see the "valley" between this present age of the church (1 Peter 1:10–12). Believers today aren't living under the curse of the Law, because Jesus bore that curse "on a tree" (Gal. 3:10–14). In Christ, believers are blessed with "every spiritual blessing" (Ephesians 1:3) because of the grace of God. For them, life means the blessings of Gerizim and not the curses of Ebal.

However, because Christians "are not under the Law, but under grace" (Romans 6:14; 7:1–6), it doesn't mean that we can live any way we please and ignore the Law of God or defy it. We aren't saved by keeping the Law, nor are we sanctified by trying to meet the demands of the Law; but "the righteousness of the Law" is "fulfilled in us" as we walk in the power of the Holy Spirit (Romans 8:4). If we put ourselves under the Law, we forfeit the enjoyment of the blessings of grace (Gal. 5). If we walk in the Spirit, we experience His life-changing power and live pleasing to God.[4]

Joshua and the Israelites did not yet have the blessing of the Spirit of God living in them through Christ, but they took God and His Law seriously in the valley between the mountains, agreeing that to read it, hear it, and obey it, was a blessing to them, just as it is to us today.

Questions:

1. After the people win the battle at Ai, they stop to worship God and hear His Word anew, refocusing on God Himself as the Giver of blessings. Are you focused on God's blessings or on God Himself?

2. How can you seek God's presence in worship through a priority on His Word? Write down specific ways you can worship Him through His Word.

3. What comes to mind when you picture this scene described at the end of Joshua 8? As you imagine the enormous crowd split in half standing with mountains to their back and facing the ark of the covenant, what would have been your reaction if you had been there?

4. Spend some time today praising Jesus for who He is through what His Word reveals.

Day Fifty-Two

Joshua

A Family around Scripture

Now this is the commandment – the statutes and the rules
– that the Lord your God commanded me to teach you, that
you may do them in the land to which you are going over, to
possess it, that you may fear the Lord your God,
you and your son and your son's son, by keeping all His
statutes and his commandments, which I command you, all the
days of your life, and that your days may be long.
Hear therefore, O Israel, and be careful to do them, that it may
go well with you, and that you may multiply greatly,
as the Lord, the God of your fathers, has promised you,
in a land flowing with milk and honey.
Deuteronomy 6:1-3

Text: Joshua 8:34-35
[34] And afterward he read all the words of the law, the blessing
and the curse, according to all that is written in the Book of the
Law. [35] There was not a word of all that Moses commanded that
Joshua did not read before all the assembly of Israel, and the
women, and the little ones, and the sojourners who lived among
them.

Thoughts:
God gave Moses the commandments so that His people
could live by them in the Promised Land. God was guiding them
into enemy land, where they would be living in a culture that
was foreign to God's ways and laws, so it was vitally important

that Israel did not conform to the world around them. They would need constant reminders of how God taught them to live. If Israel obeyed God's Word, it would go well for them. What good would it be living in the Promised Land if they lived under a curse rather than in the blessings of God?

David Jackman, in his *Preaching the Word Commentary Series*, gives some incredible comments on this last section of Joshua 8:

Everybody needs to hear the repeated revelation of the mind and will of God - men, women, children, the resident aliens including proselytes like Rahab (v. 35b). And they need to hear "all the words of the law" (v. 34). Every individual has a personal responsibility to be obedient to the terms of the covenant, and neither gender nor age nor ethnic origin is a cause for exception. There is never to be another Achan. We are not told specifically about the people's response, for only God knows the heart, but certainly no one was left in any doubt as to what the Lord required of them and how to live so as to be pleasing to him. However, the predominant note is that of blessing the people of Israel (v. 33b). Yes, the curses will have to be read and heeded, since they are the obverse side of the covenant relationship when unfaithfulness occurs; but they are not the main emphasis, nor is their avoidance the major motivation. It is the rehearsal of the blessings that is designed to win the people's gratitude and affections, so that obedience becomes the natural response of thankfulness. "Just look what can be yours if you will love the Lord your God with all your being, expressed by trust and obedience." That is the emphasis.

This is helpful as we come to see how these principles relate to us in our own day. We live in a culture that wants to be self-sufficient. We don't want to have to trust or be dependent on anybody; we want to run our own lives in our own way. We are adept at creating and worshipping any number of idols as substitutes for God, but behind them all stands the great idol of self—governing our lives with all the false confidence of creaturely pride in rebellion against the Creator. Obedience then becomes a hateful concept, since we have come to believe that no one (not even God if he exists) has the right to tell us what or what not to do. One of the most recorded popular songs in recent decades is "My Way," with its recurring line "I did it my way." So when someone is converted to Christ, a great deal of reprogramming is needed. The most fundamental Christian creed is, "Jesus Christ is Lord," which is why he can be the Savior. Yet so much contemporary evangelism either plays down or even ignores this central reality. Thus we have many who would claim Jesus as Savior and expect to enjoy all the blessings of forgiveness and peace, but who clearly are not living their daily lives with Jesus as Lord. Biblically this is not just inconsistent but ultimately impossible, since there cannot be a rescue without coming under the rescuer's rule.[1]

Questions:

1. Why do you think God had Joshua read "all the words of the law, the blessing and the curse, according to all that is written in the Book of the Law"?

2. How do you obey God's Word completely in a culture that opposes God?

3. How does Deuteronomy 6:4-9 relate to Joshua 8:34-35?

4 "Hear, O Israel: The Lord our God, the Lord is one. 5 You shall love the Lord your God with all your heart and with all your soul and with all your might. 6 And these words that I command you today shall be on your heart. 7 You shall teach them diligently to your children, and shall talk of them when you sit in your house, and when you walk by the way, and when you lie down, and when you rise. 8 You shall bind them as a sign on your hand, and they shall be as frontlets between your eyes. 9 You shall write them on the doorposts of your house and on your gates."

Day Fifty-Three

Joshua

When Evil Joins Forces

You'll face overwhelming odds; you'll be incredibly outnum-
bered. Fear would be your natural inclination.
But keep in mind, God is with you.
James S. McDonald[1]

Text: Joshua 9:1-2
[1] As soon as all the kings who were beyond the Jordan in
the hill country and in the lowland all along the coast of the
Great Sea toward Lebanon, the Hittites, the Amorites, the
Canaanites, the Perizzites, the Hivites, and the Jebusites,
heard of this, [2] they gathered together as one to fight against
Joshua and Israel.

Thoughts:
The middle region of the Promised Land is comprised of
Jericho, Ai, Gibeon, and Bethel. Israel already controls Jericho
and Ai, and Joshua is moving westward towards the other
two. Once all four cities are secured, Israel will have divided
the Promised Land in half and be able to lead campaigns into
the North and the South from this vantage point. Literally,
Joshua is leading God's people to divide and conquer.

Alan Carr, in his book *Joshua: Claiming Your Canaan*,
provides great personal application of the lessons learned in
each of Israel's battles for the central part of the Promised
Land:

The people of Israel have just defeated the city of Ai and are preparing to march deeper into Canaan as they claim the Promised Land which the Lord had given to them. As I said, they are fresh from a victory. In fact, they now have a couple of impressive victories under their belts. They have seen the great walled city of Jericho defeated and they have witnessed the pesky little town of Ai defeated too. However, before they will ever see another victory, Israel must learn a valuable lesson about becoming too friendly with the enemy.

In the battles and stories related to Israel's conquest of Canaan, we can see a picture of our lives as children of God as we struggle to obtain victory in our lives. As I look at the Bible's record of these events, it is not too hard for me to see the parallels between the battles Israel fought in the flesh and the ones which we fight in the spirit. In fact, these cities that they have faced all teach us a spiritual lesson.

Jericho—A type of the world—It was defeated, and we have the promise of victory over the world in our walk with the Lord Jesus.

Ai—A type of the flesh—It, too, was defeated, and we have the promise of victory in the flesh as we battle for the Lord Jesus Christ.

Gibeon—A type of the devil—This is a battle that still must be fought. However, we have been promised victory in this area as well. To obtain it, we must trust the Lord Jesus Christ and walk in His will day by day. The devil can be defeated.[2]

Questions:

1. How are you doing in your battle against the world, the flesh, and the devil? How do Paul's words in Ephesians 2:1-5 describe all three areas of attack, and where does Paul say your victory comes from?

> ¹And you were dead in the trespasses and sins ² in which you once walked, following the course of this world, following the prince of the power of the air, the spirit that is now at work in the sons of disobedience— ³ among whom we all once lived in the passions of our flesh, carrying out the desires of the body and the mind, and were by nature children of wrath, like the rest of mankind. ⁴ But God, being rich in mercy, because of the great love with which he loved us, ⁵ even when we were dead in our trespasses, made us alive together with Christ—by grace you have been saved . . .

2. How does 1 John 5:4 relate to your spiritual Jericho?

> ⁴ For everyone who has been born of God overcomes the world. And this is the victory that has overcome the world—our faith.

3. How does Romans 7:24-25 relate to your spiritual Ai?

> [24] Wretched man that I am! Who will deliver me from this body of death? [25] Thanks be to God through Jesus Christ our Lord! So then, I myself serve the law of God with my mind, but with my flesh I serve the law of sin.

4. How does James 4:7-10 relate to your spiritual Gibeon?

> [7] Submit yourselves therefore to God. Resist the devil, and he will flee from you. [8] Draw near to God, and he will draw near to you. Cleanse your hands, you sinners, and purify your hearts, you double-minded. [9] Be wretched and mourn and weep. Let your laughter be turned to mourning and your joy to gloom. [10] Humble yourselves before the Lord, and he will exalt you.

Day Fifty-Four

Joshua

Deception and Gullibility

A lie consists in speaking a falsehood
with the intention of deceiving.
Augustine[1]

If I speak what is false, I must answer for it.
If I speak the truth, it will answer for me.
Thomas Fuller[2]

Text: Joshua 9:3-15

[3] But when the inhabitants of Gibeon heard what Joshua had done to Jericho and to Ai, [4] they on their part acted with cunning and went and made ready provisions and took worn-out sacks for their donkeys, and wineskins, worn-out and torn and mended, [5] with worn-out, patched sandals on their feet, and worn-out clothes. And all their provisions were dry and crumbly. [6] And they went to Joshua in the camp at Gilgal and said to him and to the men of Israel, "We have come from a distant country, so now make a covenant with us." [7] But the men of Israel said to the Hivites, "Perhaps you live among us; then how can we make a covenant with you?" [8] They said to Joshua, "We are your servants." And Joshua said to them, "Who are you? And where do you come from?" [9] They said to him, "From a very distant country your servants have come, because of the name of the Lord your God. For we have heard a report of him, and all that he did in Egypt, [10] and all that he did to the two kings of the Amorites who were beyond

the Jordan, to Sihon the king of Heshbon, and to Og king of Bashan, who lived in Ashtaroth. ¹¹ So our elders and all the inhabitants of our country said to us, 'Take provisions in your hand for the journey and go to meet them and say to them, "We are your servants. Come now, make a covenant with us."' ¹² Here is our bread. It was still warm when we took it from our houses as our food for the journey on the day we set out to come to you, but now, behold, it is dry and crumbly.

¹³ These wineskins were new when we filled them, and behold, they have burst. And these garments and sandals of ours are worn out from the very long journey." ¹⁴ So the men took some of their provisions, but did not ask counsel from the Lord. ¹⁵ And Joshua made peace with them and made a covenant with them, to let them live, and the leaders of the congregation swore to them.

Thoughts:

In Joshua 9, the pagan kings throughout the land join forces to fend off the Israelite invaders. But the tribe of Gibeon devised a different approach. The Gibeonites develop a scheme of deception. But you would think that Joshua and the nation of Israel would be so dependent on God at this point that God would intervene. Notice verse 14 of our text.

¹⁴ So the men took some of their provisions, **but did not ask counsel from the Lord**.

These bolded words signal trouble ahead. Here we see the danger of trusting in ourselves. Some of our biggest problems come from not seeking God in every circumstance, and this was certainly the case for Israel.

The Gibeonites use cunning deception and play on Joshua and the leaders' implied (and understandable) desire to avoid unnecessary conflict. Charles Swindoll tells an interesting story about a similarly cunning man who scraped the side of a car while parking late at night, in front of several witnesses. Swindoll says that the man "took out a piece of paper and he wrote on it, 'A number of people around me think I'm leaving you a note that includes my name and address, but I'm not.'"[3]

Put more generally, innocent and trusting people – like the bystanders who saw the car get scratched – can be fooled into believing false information that appears credible. When Israel's enemies, the Gibeonites, come in with complete trickery, they are a picture of how our enemy, the devil, works: he is a master deceiver who plays on a fraction of the truth to get us to swallow a big lie.

Joshua made peace with his enemies because he believed their lies based on evidence that looked real to him. There is much confusion today in our culture about what is real and what is fake, and there are pretenders everywhere. The best way to avoid being tricked by what deceivers say is to know what God's Word says, and to ask God to show you what is real and true. As Proverbs 3:5-6 tells us:

> [5] Trust in the LORD with all your heart, and do not lean on your own understanding. [6] In all your ways acknowledge him, and he will make straight your paths.

Let us never forget that our God is the source of all wisdom and truth. When the path before us is full of enemies and hidden traps, remember to ask God for His guidance, because He is always faithful to give it.

Questions:

1. In what ways do you see deception in our world today?

2. In what ways have you made peace with the devil because you did not recognize him for who he is?

3. How does John 10:10 reveal both Satan's and God's true intentions?

> The thief comes only to steal and kill and destroy.
> I came that they may have life and have it abundantly.

Day Fifty-Five

Joshua

Maintain Your Integrity at Any Cost

Integrity is keeping my commitment even if the circumstances
when I made the commitment have changed.
David Jeremiah[1]

Text: Joshua 9:16-21

[16] At the end of three days after they had made a covenant
with them, they heard that they were their neighbors and that
they lived among them. [17] And the people of Israel set out and
reached their cities on the third day. Now their cities were
Gibeon, Chephirah, Beeroth, and Kiriath-jearim. [18] But the
people of Israel did not attack them, because the leaders of the
congregation had sworn to them by the Lord, the God of Israel.
Then all the congregation murmured against the leaders. [19] But
all the leaders said to all the congregation, "We have sworn to
them by the Lord, the God of Israel, and now we may not touch
them. [20] This we will do to them: let them live, lest wrath be
upon us, because of the oath that we swore to them." [21] And the
leaders said to them, "Let them live." So they became cutters of
wood and drawers of water for all the congregation, just as the
leaders had said of them.

Thoughts:

Remember at the end of Joshua 8, the army of Israel has
conquered the city of Ai. In gratitude to God, Joshua builds an
altar on Mount Ebal. He offers sacrifices, reads the Law of Moses
to the people, and reaffirms Israel's covenant with the Lord. In

summary, Joshua and the people have just experienced a spiritual revival. They have rededicated themselves to God and have pledged obedience to His Word.

The Israelites have gone through a "mountaintop experience" – and mountaintops can be spiritual danger zones. We should always be watchful immediately after a spiritual victory. The euphoria of a mountaintop experience can make us vulnerable to spiritual deception. Many sincere Christians have fallen prey to Satan's traps immediately after a spiritual highpoint.

Paul wrote these words to the Corinthians in 1 Corinthians 10:12: "Therefore let anyone who thinks that he stands take heed lest he fall." When you think you have it made, watch out!! That's precisely when you are most vulnerable to Satan's attack. Don't be surprised if you suddenly experience opposition and deception just as you begin to be effective for Jesus. Satan is watching for signs of weakness, and he wants to block God's power in our lives.

The New Testament tells us in James 1:5, "If any of you lacks wisdom, let him ask God, who gives generously to all without reproach, and it will be given him." Notice the Bible doesn't say that God may give you wisdom. It says God will give it to you – generously and in abundance. And I love the "without reproach" part. That means He won't fuss at you when you finally come and ask. That's a promise from God. So don't forget to ask. And don't be afraid to ask. Make sure you have received God's direction for daily decisions.

We know that Joshua and the leaders failed to ask God for wisdom before making promises to the Gibeonites, but they act with extreme integrity in upholding their word to the Gibeonites once they had given it. In David Guzik's words, "It is a mark of godliness to hold to an oath, even when it is difficult."[2] When we make a promise, we must find a way to honor God and keep our word.

Former senator John Ashcroft, in *Lessons from a Father to His Sons*, tells a great story about keeping your word that occurred in the life of basketball great Michael Jordan.

> Until 1997 Michael Jordan, indisputably the leading player in the NBA for over a decade, was never the highest-paid player. When asked why he did not do what so many other players do—hold out on their contracts until they get more money—Michael replied, "I have always honored my word. I went for security. I had six-year contracts, and I always honored them. People said I was underpaid, but when I signed on the dotted line, I gave my word."
>
> Three years later, after several highly visible players reneged on their contracts, a reporter asked Michael once again about being underpaid, and he explained that if his kids saw their dad breaking a promise, how could he continue training them to keep their word? By not asking for a contract renegotiation, Michael Jordan spoke volumes to his children. He told them, "You stand by your word, even when that might go against you." His silence became a roar.[3]

Michael Jordan's position echoes the one taken millennia before by Joshua and the leaders of the Israelites.

I believe that God honored Joshua's faithfulness to keep his word. While God was not pleased that Joshua failed to seek His wisdom in the matter, God always honors people when they are true to their word. We all know the saying, "Two wrongs don't make a right." Someone else's deception doesn't give you an excuse to go back on your word.

Questions:

1. In what ways are you prone to lowering your integrity because someone else has lied to you? How difficult do you think it was for Joshua to maintain his integrity when his betrayal was known and criticized by his own people?

2. Considering today's devotion, what are your thoughts on Colossians 3:9?

> ⁹ Do not lie to one another, seeing that you have put off the old self with its practices . . .

3. What spiritual application does James 5:12 add to today's lesson?

> ¹² But above all, my brothers, do not swear, either by heaven or by earth or by any other oath, but let your "yes" be yes and your "no" be no, so that you may not fall under condemnation.

Day Fifty-Six

Joshua

Do the Right Thing

Always do what is right. It will gratify half of mankind
and astound the other.
Mark Twain[1]

Text: Joshua 9:22-27

[22] Joshua summoned them, and he said to them, "Why did you deceive us, saying, 'We are very far from you,' when you dwell among us? [23] Now therefore you are cursed, and some of you shall never be anything but servants, cutters of wood and drawers of water for the house of my God." [24] They answered Joshua, "Because it was told to your servants for a certainty that the Lord your God had commanded his servant Moses to give you all the land and to destroy all the inhabitants of the land from before you—so we feared greatly for our lives because of you and did this thing. [25] And now, behold, we are in your hand. Whatever seems good and right in your sight to do to us, do it." [26] So he did this to them and delivered them out of the hand of the people of Israel, and they did not kill them. [27] But Joshua made them that day cutters of wood and drawers of water for the congregation and for the altar of the Lord, to this day, in the place that he should choose.

Thoughts:

Martin Luther King, Jr. once said, "It is always the right time to do the right thing." Someone else said, "Do what is right, not what is easy." I once heard it said, "The softest pillow is a clean conscience."

Joshua had a choice to make. He was deceived by the Gibeonites and made a peace treaty with them. He was lied to and deceived, yet he still had the opportunity to do the right thing.

In Joshua 9:24, the Gibeonites gave their reason for deceiving Joshua: They feared for their lives. Now, remember we never have a valid reason for lying. When we follow God, the truth always leads to a righteous life.

I find the Gibeonites' reason and response very insightful. They would rather lie and live than tell the truth and die. They do the wrong thing and get caught. Yet in verse 25, they tell Joshua to do what seems good and right. Isn't it just like our selfish nature to give in to evil but expect other people to do what is right? We don't mind lying to others, but we believe other people should deal honestly with us.

Joshua does what is right. He keeps his word and delivers them. He keeps his peace treaty but also gives them jobs to do as they join God's people. At the time of the deception, the Gibeonites didn't believe in Israel's God. However, their new jobs involved cutting wood and drawing water for the altar of the Lord. Joshua assigns them tough jobs that would remind them of their deceit. And at the same time, He assigns them tasks involved in the rituals of worshipping God so that they can turn and trust in Jehovah. Joshua took a bad situation and used it for the glory of God.

When we are wronged or do wrong, we need to surrender to God's will for the next right step in our journey with Jesus. Your failures do not have to defeat you. God's grace is greater than any of your mistakes. If we do the right thing in our present circumstances, God can bring restoration and redemption for our future. Remember we serve a God who brings dead things back to life again! He has no trouble bringing victory from defeat. No matter what you've done, or where you've been, just do the next right thing!

Questions:

1. Describe a time when you were wronged but still chose to do the right thing.

2. How does doing the right thing in a bad situation give a greater testimony of your faith in Jesus Christ?

3. How do you think God's command in Deuteronomy 6:18 impacted Joshua's response to the Gibeonites?

> [18] And you shall do what is right and good in the sight of the Lord, that it may go well with you, and that you may go in and take possession of the good land that the Lord swore to give to your fathers . . .

4. What are your thoughts on Mark Twain's quote that started today's devotion?

Joshua

Notes

Introduction
[1] Gangel, Kenneth O. 2002. *Joshua*. Edited by Max Anders. Holman Old Testament Commentary. B&H Publishing Group.
[2] Peckham, Colin N. 2007. *Joshua: A Devotional Commentary*. Exploring the Bible Commentary. Leominster, UK: Day One Publications.
[3] Gangel, Kenneth O. 2002. *Joshua*. Edited by Max Anders. Holman Old Testament Commentary. B&H Publishing Group.
[4] Howard, David M., Jr. 1998. *Joshua*. Vol. 5. The New American Commentary. Nashville: Broadman & Holman Publishers.
[5] Wiersbe, Warren W. 1996. *Be Strong*. "Be" Commentary Series. Wheaton, IL: Victor Books.
[6] Lennox, Stephen J. 2015. *Joshua: A Commentary in the Wesleyan Tradition*. Edited by Alex Varughese, Roger Hahn, and George Lyons. New Beacon Bible Commentary. Kansas City: Beacon Hill Press.

Day 1
[1] Howard, David M., Jr. 1998. *Joshua*. Vol. 5. The New American Commentary. Nashville: Broadman & Holman Publishers.
[2] Harbour, Brian L. 2008. *Joshua*. Notable Harbour In-Depth Studies. WORDsearch.
[3] Lucado, Max. 2015. *Glory Days: Trusting the God Who Fights for You*. Nashville: Thomas Nelson.

Day 2

[1] Jackman, David. 2014. *Joshua: People of God's Purpose*. Edited by R. Kent Hughes. Preaching the Word. Wheaton, IL: Crossway.
[2] Lucado, Max. 2015. *Glory Days: Trusting the God Who Fights for You*. Nashville: Thomas Nelson.
[3] Jackman, David. 2014. *Joshua: People of God's Purpose*. Edited by R. Kent Hughes. Preaching the Word. Wheaton, IL: Crossway.

Day 3

[1] Sweeting, George. 1995. *Who Said That? More than 2,500 Usable Quotes and Illustrations*. Chicago, IL: Moody Publishers.
[2] Harbour, Brian L. 2008. *Joshua*. Notable Harbour In-Depth Studies. WORDsearch.
[3] Francis A. Schaeffer, *Joshua and the Flow of Biblical History* (Downers Grove, IL: InterVarsity Press, 1975), 34.
[4] Carr, Alan. 2012. *Joshua: Claiming Your Canaan*. The Topical Sermon Notebook. WORDsearch; Cross.

Day 4

[1] Mathews, Kenneth A. 2016. *Joshua*. Edited by Mark L. Strauss and John H. Walton. Teach the Text Commentary Series. Grand Rapids, MI: Baker Books: A Division of Baker Publishing Group.
[2] Lucado, Max. 2015. *Glory Days: Trusting the God Who Fights for You*. Nashville: Thomas Nelson.
[3] Davis, Dale Ralph. 2000. *Joshua: No Falling Words*. Focus on the Bible Commentary. Scotland: Christian Focus Publications.

Day 5

[1] Barnes A. (2019, November 7). *211 quotes about obedience*. ChristianQuotes.info. https://www.christianquotes.info/quotes-by-topic/quotes-about-obedience/

[2] Smith, Robert, Jr. 2023. *Exalting Jesus in Joshua*. Edited by David Platt, Daniel L. Akin, and Tony Merida. Christ-Centered Exposition Commentary. Brentwood, TN: Holman Reference.

Day 6
[1] Piper, J. (n.d.). *Top 25 Christian living quotes (of 65): A-Z quotes.* A. https://www.azquotes.com/quotes/topics/christian-living.html
[2] Carr, Alan. 2012. *Joshua: Claiming Your Canaan*. The Topical Sermon Notebook. WORDsearch; Cross.

Day 7
[1] Elliot J. (2019, November 7). *211 quotes about obedience.* ChristianQuotes.info. https://www.christianquotes.info/quotes-by-topic/quotes-about-obedience/
[2] Huffman, Jr., John A., and Lloyd J. Ogilvie. 1986. *Joshua*. Vol. 6. The Preacher's Commentary Series. Nashville, TN: Thomas Nelson Inc.

Day 8
[1] Boice, James Montgomery. 2005. *Joshua*. Grand Rapids, MI: Baker Books.
[2] Mathews, Kenneth A. 2016. *Joshua*. Edited by Mark L. Strauss and John H. Walton. Teach the Text Commentary Series. Grand Rapids, MI: Baker Books: A Division of Baker Publishing Group.
[3] Lucado, Max. 2015. *Glory Days: Trusting the God Who Fights for You*. Nashville: Thomas Nelson.
[4] Wiersbe, Warren W. 1996. *Be Strong*. "Be" Commentary Series. Wheaton, IL: Victor Books.

Day 9

[1] Morgan, Robert J. 2000. *Nelson's Complete Book of Stories, Illustrations, and Quotes*. Electronic ed. Nashville: Thomas Nelson Publishers.

[2] Gangel, Kenneth O. 2002. *Joshua*. Edited by Max Anders. Holman Old Testament Commentary. B&H Publishing Group.

[3] Davis, Dale Ralph. 2000. *Joshua: No Falling Words*. Focus on the Bible Commentary. Scotland: Christian Focus Publications.

[4] Hubbard, Robert L., Jr. 2009. *Joshua*. The NIV Application Commentary. Grand Rapids, MI: Zondervan.

[5] Gangel, Kenneth O. 2002. *Joshua*. Edited by Max Anders. Holman Old Testament Commentary. B&H Publishing Group.

[6] Hubbard, Robert L., Jr. 2009. *Joshua*. The NIV Application Commentary. Grand Rapids, MI: Zondervan.

Day 10

[1] Wiersbe, Warren W. 1996. *Be Strong*. "Be" Commentary Series. Wheaton, IL: Victor Books.

[2] Howard, David M., Jr. 1998. *Joshua*. Vol. 5. The New American Commentary. Nashville: Broadman & Holman Publishers.

[3] Wiersbe, Warren W. 1996. *Be Strong*. "Be" Commentary Series. Wheaton, IL: Victor Books.

Day 11

[1] Pitkänen, Pekka M. A. 2010. *Joshua*. Edited by David W. Baker and Gordon J. Wenham. Vol. 6. Apollos Old Testament Commentary. Nottingham, England; Downers Grove, IL: Apollos; InterVarsity Press.

[2] Jackman, David. 2014. *Joshua: People of God's Purpose*. Edited by R. Kent Hughes. Preaching the Word. Wheaton, IL: Crossway.

[3] Mounce, William D. 2006. In *Mounce's Complete Expository Dictionary of Old & New Testament Words*, 378. Grand Rapids, MI: Zondervan.

Day 12
[1] Rhodes, Ron. 2011. *1001 Unforgettable Quotes about God, Faith, & the Bible*. Eugene, OR: Harvest House Publishers.

Day 13
[1] Morgan, Robert J. 2000. *Nelson's Complete Book of Stories, Illustrations, and Quotes*. Electronic ed. Nashville: Thomas Nelson Publishers.

Day 14
[1] Wray Beal, Lissa M. 2019. *Joshua*. Edited by Tremper Longman III. The Story of God Bible Commentary. Grand Rapids, MI: Zondervan Academic.

Day 15
[1] Jackman, David. 2014. *Joshua: People of God's Purpose*. Edited by R. Kent Hughes. Preaching the Word. Wheaton, IL: Crossway.
[2] Lennox, Stephen J. 2015. *Joshua: A Commentary in the Wesleyan Tradition*. Edited by Alex Varughese, Roger Hahn, and George Lyons. New Beacon Bible Commentary. Kansas City: Beacon Hill Press.

Day 16
[1] Heitzig, S. (n.d.-c). *Joshua 3-4 - Skipheitzig.com teaching*. http://skipheitzig.com/teachings_view. asp?ServiceID=4181&transcript=1#transcript
[2] Redpath, Alan. 1955. *Victorious Christian Living*. Westwood, NJ: Fleming H. Revell Company, 52-53.
[3] Ibid, 54.

Day 17
[1] Gangel, Kenneth O. 2002. *Joshua*. Edited by Max Anders. Holman Old Testament Commentary. B&H Publishing Group.

Day 18
[1] Boice, James Montgomery. 2005. *Joshua*. Grand Rapids, MI: Baker Books.

Day 19
[1] Walden, K., & By. (2020, January 4). *Battle Archives*. Daily Christian Quotes. https://www.dailychristianquote.com/tag/battle/
[2] Maxwell, L. (n.d.). *10 spiritual battle quotes for real warriors*. Prayers and Promises. https://dianarasmussen.com/10-spiritual-battle-quotes-for-real-warriors/

Day 20
[1] TerKeurst, L. (n.d.). *Cultivating a heart that says "yes" to god*. Proverbs 31 Ministries. https://proverbs31.org/read/devotions/full-post/2023/06/15/cultivating-a-heart-that-says-yes-to-god

Day 22
[1] Wesley, J. (n.d.). *Top 25 quotes by John Wesley (of 200): A-Z quotes*. azquotes.com. Retrieved January 22, 2023, from https://www.azquotes.com/author/15507-John_Wesley

Day 23
[1] Nelson, R. M. (n.d.). *Top 25 covenant quotes (of 303): A-Z quotes*. https://www.azquotes.com/quotes/topics/covenant.html

Day 24
[1] Wesley, J. (n.d.). *Top 25 quotes by John Wesley (of 200): A-Z quotes*.
azquotes.com. Retrieved January 22, 2023, from
https://www.azquotes.com/author/15507-John_Wesley

Day 25
[1] 2011. *Every Day with Jesus: Treasures from the Greatest Christian Writers of All Time*. New York, NY: Worthy Books.

Day 26
[1] Walden, K. (2022, August 20). *Shame archives*. Daily Christian Quotes. https://www.dailychristianquote.com/tag/shame/

Day 27
[1] https://www.ibelieve.com/faith/inspiring-quotes-gods-timing.html
[2] Harbour, Brian L. 2008. *Joshua*. Notable Harbour In-Depth Studies. WORDsearch.
[3] Howard, David M., Jr. 1998. *Joshua*. Vol. 5. The New American Commentary. Nashville: Broadman & Holman Publishers.

Day 28
[1] Sayings, F. Q. &. (n.d.). *Top 72 quotes about god's provision: Famous quotes & sayings about god's provision*. Famous Quotes & Sayings. https://quotestats.com/topic/quotes-about-gods-provision/

Day 29
[1] Lucado, Max. 2015. *Glory Days: Trusting the God Who Fights for You*. Nashville: Thomas Nelson.
[2] Ibid.
[3] Ibid.

Day 30

[1] Warren W. Wiersbe, *Real Worship: Playground, Battleground, or Holy Ground?* (Grand Rapids, MI: Baker Books, 2000), 29.
[2] Davis, Dale Ralph. 2000. *Joshua: No Falling Words*. Focus on the Bible Commentary. Scotland: Christian Focus Publications.
[3] Lawson, Steven J. 2010. "Chapter 3: 'The Holy One of God': The Holiness of Jesus." In *Holy, Holy, Holy: Proclaiming the Perfections of God*, 35. Lake Mary, FL: Reformation Trust Publishing.

Day 31

[1] Huffman, Jr., John A., and Lloyd J. Ogilvie. 1986. *Joshua*. Vol. 6. The Preacher's Commentary Series. Nashville, TN: Thomas Nelson Inc.
[2] Lucado, Max. 2015. *Glory Days: Trusting the God Who Fights for You*. Nashville: Thomas Nelson.
[3] Gangel, Kenneth O. 2002. *Joshua*. Edited by Max Anders. Holman Old Testament Commentary. B&H Publishing Group.

Day 32

[1] Butler, John G. 1996. *Joshua: The Conqueror of Canaan*. Vol. Number Thirteen. Bible Biography Series. Clinton, IA: LBC Publications.

Day 33

[1] Jackman, David. 2014. *Joshua: People of God's Purpose*. Edited by R. Kent Hughes. Preaching the Word. Wheaton, IL: Crossway.

Day 34

[1] Sayings, F. Q. &. (n.d.). *Top 72 quotes about god's provision: Famous quotes & sayings about god's provision*. Famous Quotes & Sayings. https://quotestats.com/topic/quotes-about-gods-provision/

Day 35

[1] Butler, John G. 1996. *Joshua: The Conqueror of Canaan*. Vol. Number Thirteen. Bible Biography Series. Clinton, IA: LBC Publications.

Day 36

[1] Osbeck, Kenneth W. 1985. *101 More Hymn Stories*. Grand Rapids, MI: Kregel Publications.
[2] Ibid.

Day 37

[1] Wellman, P. J. (2019c, December 18). *20 awesome quotes about Salvation*. ChristianQuotes.info. https://www.christianquotes.info/top-quotes/20-awesome-quotes-salvation/
[2] Quinitchett, K. (2023, May 22). *1972 Uruguayan Air Force Flight 571: What to know about the crash survivors*. The US Sun. https://www.the-sun.com/news/8179152/uruguayan-air-force-flight-571-andes-plane-crash-survivors/
[3] Colón, P. (n.d.). *Archaeology confirms the walls "fell flat."* Israel My Glory. https://israelmyglory.org/article/archaeology-confirms-the-walls-fell-flat/

Day 38

[1] Heitzig, S. (n.d.-e). *Joshua 5-6 - Skipheitzig.com teaching*. http://skipheitzig.com/teachings_view.asp?ServiceID=4183&transcript=1#transcript

Day 39

[1] Boice, James Montgomery. 2005. *Joshua*. Grand Rapids, MI: Baker Books.

Day 40

[1] Nee, W. (n.d.). *Top 25 overconfident quotes: A-Z quotes*. A. https://www.azquotes.com/quotes/topics/overconfident.html

[2] Coach, P. (2018, June 8). *20 Wesley Duewel quotes on prayer*. prayer coach. https://prayer-coach.com/prayer-quote-wesley-duewel/

[3] Carr, Alan. 2012. *Joshua: Claiming Your Canaan*. The Topical Sermon Notebook. WORDsearch; Cross.

Day 41

[1] Barnhouse, Donald. *Top 30 quotes about consequences of sin: Famous quotes & sayings about consequences of sin*. Famous Quotes & Sayings. https://quotestats.com/topic/quotes-about-consequences-of-sin/

Day 42

[1] Sayings, F. Q. &. (n.d.). *Top 72 quotes about god's provision: Famous quotes & sayings about god's provision*. Famous Quotes & Sayings. https://quotestats.com/topic/quotes-about-gods-provision/

Day 43

[1] Wellman, P. J. (2015b, December 28). *40 quotes about responsibility*. ChristianQuotes.info. https://www.christianquotes.info/quotes-by-topic/quotes-about-responsibility/

[2] Firth, David G. 2021. *Joshua*. Edited by T. Desmond Alexander, Thomas R. Schreiner, and Andreas J. Köstenberger. Evangelical Biblical Theology Commentary. Bellingham, WA: Lexham Press.

[3] Peckham, Colin N. 2007. *Joshua: A Devotional Commentary*. Exploring the Bible Commentary. Leominster, UK: Day One Publications.

Day 44
[1] Fitzgerald, F. S. (n.d.). *Top 10 God knows everything quotes: A-Z quotes*. https://www.azquotes.com/quotes/topics/God-knows-everything.html
[2] DeYoung, Kevin. (n.d.). *Top 10 God knows everything quotes: A-Z quotes*. https://www.azquotes.com/quotes/topics/God-knows-everything.html

Day 45
[1] *Top 25 covetousness quotes (of 108): A-Z quotes*. A. (n.d.). https://www.azquotes.com/quotes/topics/covetousness.html
[2] Ibid.
[3] Huffman, Jr., John A., and Lloyd J. Ogilvie. 1986. *Joshua*. Vol. 6. The Preacher's Commentary Series. Nashville, TN: Thomas Nelson Inc.
[4] Peckham, Colin N. 2007. *Joshua: A Devotional Commentary*. Exploring the Bible Commentary. Leominster, UK: Day One Publications.

Day 46
[1] Wiersbe, Warren W. 1996. *Be Strong*. "Be" Commentary Series. Wheaton, IL: Victor Books.

Day 47
[1] Warren, R. (n.d.). 40 Christian quotes to inspire your faith every day – parade. https://parade.com/living/christian-quotes
[2] Guzik, David. 2000. *Joshua*. David Guzik's Commentaries on the Bible. Santa Barbara, CA: David Guzik.

[3] Peckham, Colin N. 2007. *Joshua: A Devotional Commentary*. Exploring the Bible Commentary. Leominster, UK: Day One Publications.

Day 48
[1] Wellman, P. J. (2015, December 28). *30 quotes about failure*. ChristianQuotes.info. https://www.christianquotes.info/quotes-by-topic/quotes-about-failure/
[2] Bargh, E. (2022, October 10). *4 lessons only failure can teach*. YMI. https://ymi.today/2017/11/4-lessons-only-failure-can-teach/
[3] Ibid.

Day 49
[1] Howard, David M., Jr. 1998. *Joshua*. Vol. 5. The New American Commentary. Nashville: Broadman & Holman Publishers.

Day 50
[1] Greear, J.D. (n.d.). *Top 25 altars quotes (of 407): A-z quotes*. A. https://www.azquotes.com/quotes/topics/altars.html
[2] Hadley, B. (2021, October 26). *19 inspiring quotes about worship*. MediaShout. https://mediashout.com/inspiring-worship-quotes/
[3] Peckham, Colin N. 2007. *Joshua: A Devotional Commentary*. Exploring the Bible Commentary. Leominster, UK: Day One Publications.

Day 51
[1] Zuck, Roy B. 1997. *The Speaker's Quote Book: Over 4,500 Illustrations and Quotations for All Occasions*. Grand Rapids, MI: Kregel Publications.
[2] Lucado, Max. 2015. *Glory Days: Trusting the God Who Fights for You*. Nashville: Thomas Nelson.

[3] Harbour, Brian L. 2008. *Joshua*. Notable Harbour In-Depth Studies. WORDsearch.

[4] Wiersbe, Warren W. 1996. *Be Strong*. "Be" Commentary Series. Wheaton, IL: Victor Books.

Day 52

[1] Jackman, David. 2014. *Joshua: People of God's Purpose*. Edited by R. Kent Hughes. Preaching the Word. Wheaton, IL: Crossway.

Day 53

[1] MacDonald, J. S. (n.d.). *13 Christian quotes & sayings by James S MacDonald (quotations)*. All Christian Quotes. https://www.allchristianquotes.org/authors/120/James_S_MacDonald/

[2] Carr, Alan. 2012. *Joshua: Claiming Your Canaan*. The Topical Sermon Notebook. WORDsearch; Cross.

Day 54

[1] Wellman, P. J. (2015a, December 23). *42 quotes about lying*. ChristianQuotes.info. https://www.christianquotes.info/quotes-by-topic/quotes-about-lying/

[2] Ibid.

[3] Swindoll, Charles R. 2016. *The Tale of the Tardy Oxcart and 1501 Other Stories*. Nashville, TN: Thomas Nelson.

Day 55

[1] Rowell, Edward, ed. 2008. *1001 Quotes, Illustrations, and Humorous Stories: For Preachers, Teachers and Writers*. Baker Publishing Group.

[2] Guzik, David. 2000. *Joshua*. David Guzik's Commentaries on the Bible. Santa Barbara, CA: David Guzik.

[3] PreachingToday.com. 2002. *Perfect Illustrations: For Every Topic and Occasion*. Wheaton, IL: Tyndale House Publishers, Inc.

Day 56

[1] Twain, M. (n.d.). *Doing the right thing quotes (69 quotes)*. Goodreads. https://www.goodreads.com/quotes/tag/doing-the-right-thing

Made in the USA
Columbia, SC
15 March 2024

32798871R00143